Henry Aimé Ouvry

Stein and His Reforms in Prussia

With reference to the land question in England and an appendix containing the views of Richard Cobden and J.S. Mill's advice to land reformers

Henry Aimé Ouvry

Stein and His Reforms in Prussia
With reference to the land question in England and an appendix containing the views of Richard Cobden and J.S. Mill's advice to land reformers

ISBN/EAN: 9783337169411

Printed in Europe, USA, Canada, Australia, Japan

Cover: Foto ©Suzi / pixelio.de

More available books at **www.hansebooks.com**

STEIN AND HIS REFORMS
IN PRUSSIA,

WITH REFERENCE TO

THE LAND QUESTION IN ENGLAND:

AND AN APPENDIX CONTAINING THE VIEWS OF

RICHARD COBDEN,

AND

J. S. MILL'S ADVICE TO LAND REFORMERS.

BY

COL. H. A. OUVRY, C.B.,

MEMBER OF THE COBDEN CLUB.

"Woe unto them that join house to house, that lay field to field, till there be no place, that they may be placed alone in the midst of the earth."—ISAIAH, v. 8.

LONDON:
KERBY AND ENDEAN, 190, OXFORD STREET.
1873.

(All rights reserved.)

LONDON:
PRINTED BY KERBY AND ENDEAN,
190, OXFORD STREET.

PREFACE.

THE object of this small volume is to furnish a trustworthy account of the real nature of the Stein-Hardenberg Reforms, concerning which much misapprehension exists in England.

It is generally supposed that Stein took the part of the people against an oppressive aristocracy, but this is a great error. The truth is that he was essentially an aristocrat, and looked upon the people as (to use his own expression) the "swinish multitude" (Appendix A).

The reason why he worked for the emancipation of the Prussian peasant was simply because he wanted to make use of him as an instrument for the re-establishment of German independence. Had the Prussians been victorious in their wars with the French, most certainly we never should have heard of the Stein Reforms.

The rising tide of democracy in England is now a great fact, and as the lords of the manors and large landed proprietors thought fit to deprive the body of the people of their just right to the soil in the great agrarian revolution at the commencement of the sixteenth century, when enclosures were first made (B), there is now no element of any sufficient weight to bar its course.

The question as to the best form of government has been ably discussed in a German work lately published (C); but whatever difference of opinion there may be among the several classes of politicians, one thing is very certain, that the old ecclesiastical and political system of tutelage, in which the power of the State was vested in one person, and having for its motto "everything for the people, but nothing by the people," has died a natural death, and can never be resuscitated.

The old faith in divine right has faded away before the new light of modern thought; unreasoning faith and blind acceptation of tradition has paled before the increased intelligence and discoveries of modern science, and henceforward the task of the legislator will be to fit and accommodate all old institutions so as to meet the new state of things which must in the near future rule in Europe; and with us in England the first and most important consideration will be, how the people are to be restored to the soil from which they were driven by cruel oppression in former times; for without a class of small proprietors firmly planted on the land there can be no guarantee for the stability and greatness of the nation. The food produce of the land has always proved to be much greater under small cultivation, but were this not so, that would be of secondary consideration, for the question is far less of the absolute quantity that the soil can be made to produce than of the far more important one of forming a sound, healthy, and moral population. If it really can be proved that cultivation on a large scale is so far superior that it must be resorted to, then the system of co-operation may be brought into play, which would entirely meet the requirement, and at the same time give the people the benefit of small proprietorships and a stake in the country, by *property in the land,* and thus form them into a class of good *conservative* citizens, for when persons have no property they become dangerous to the State, as Schiller most justly observes :

> " The man of property bereft
> Will rush to murder and to theft."

Thinking men (who are not large landed proprietors) begin to see that there is a natural law by which the land of a country belongs to the State in trust for the good of the whole community, and should never be regarded as a mere chattel. These views are gaining ground universally, even in Australia, where a land reform league has been formed to prevent the alienation of the land, and to repurchase all that has already become private property. The following are the views published at Melbourne in an Electoral address—*Argus,* Jan. 3rd, 1868 :—

" On the land question I am of opinion that the State should be the sole landlord, and that it is contrary to the soundest economic, social, and political principles for the State to alienate the land. I do not see any subject of political activity equal to this for thoroughly meeting the ' condition of the people ' question, and aiding to solve the problem of what will enable the State to contribute its share towards helping the ' poor who are getting poorer,' *not by degrading eleemosynary gifts,* but by offering to earnest and willing humanity the most favourable possible surroundings for its sphere of labour and utility."

According to the doctrine of the great founder of the Median faith, no sooner does Ormuzd, the principle of beneficence, propose a new scheme for the happiness and improvement of mankind, than his opponent Ahriman immediately creates an opposition.

Ahriman is no vain imagination of the enthusiast, he lives and works at the present day as actively as of old; the father of evil, the source of darkness and impurity still violently and persistently opposes all the efforts of the children of light who are constantly striving for the perfection of the human race. That Ormuzd will, in the end, conquer there can be little doubt, but still it would be useless to deny that his opponent has great power, and that the victory will only be gained after a long and painful struggle.

If we review the great French Revolution, we find that this principle of evil, represented by the atheistic Red Republicans of the Marat stamp, opposed and impeded all the sound and wholesome reforms of those children of light, the Girondists, and succeeded in establishing an unnatural restlessness and intoxication, which gave rise to an almost unexampled orgy of crime and folly. Naturally, a violent reaction took place; under the influence of which the new birth miscarried, and freedom in Europe submitted to the despotic rule of a soldier of fortune.

Who can doubt that a Republic administered by the people is, theoretically, the most perfect form of government, but then it requires a people who are fit and prepared to govern themselves; when this condition is wanting, experience has shown that it is the very worst.

Cicero has truly remarked, " Respublica, res est populi cum bene ac juste geritur, sive ab uno rege, sive a paucis magnatibus, sive ab universo populo "—*i.e.*, a Republic is the affairs of the People administered with justice and wisdom, whether by a single ruler, a few magnates, or by the people themselves.

If the affairs of the people be administered in an unjust and tyrannical spirit, such a state of things is no republic but a tyranny, and this tyranny remains the same whether it be acted under the auspices of a King, an oligarchy, or the people themselves.

If we apply these sound principles to ourselves in England, and compare our Republic, nominally under one ruler, with the Republic of France, nominally under the rule of the people, and then examine well the state of liberty, justice, and wisdom of rule which prevails in each country, I venture to think that there are very few who would wish to change our condition for that of our neighbour.

No person, who has a grain of common sense in his composition, would have the folly to assert that the People of England are, even nearly, fit or prepared for a Republic administered by themselves; those therefore who shout for such a Republic do not really understand the meaning of the word, and may be classed among the retrograde obstructives who preach doctrines subversive of all progress, some of them even going so far as to meditate an attack on the rights of property, on a belief in God, and even on civilization itself.

No sooner is any sound and wholesome reform proposed than these obstructives come forward, and, in particular, disturb public meetings with insane and revolutionary propositions utterly undesired by the people and impracticable in themselves, thus playing the game of the Tory absolutists, and obstructing all true Reformers in their efforts for the public good.

That eventually there may be established a great European Republic I most sincerely hope and believe; and when the people of Europe are prepared for it, nothing more desirable can well be imagined. But until that time comes, it behoves all good Reformers to hold to the form of government which they possess, and to make the best of that; as a distinguished statesman recently observed, we may safely leave the other to our posterity.

Land Tenure Reform is now the great question

in this country; the stone has been set rolling, and if the people are wise they will not let it rest till a thorough radical reform has been accomplished.

H. A. OUVRY.

STEIN AND HIS REFORMS IN PRUSSIA.

BEFORE we proceed to examine the nature of the great reforms of Baron Stein, it will first be necessary to take a very cursory review of the state of Germany during the latter half of the eighteenth century.

The history of man, like the great ocean, has its periods of ebb and flow, although the tides of the one may be measured by centuries, that of the other merely by a few hours. For a more or less lengthened period, nations seem to rest inertly, as far as regards political change; being solely busied with the cares of obtaining the common necessaries of life, they pursue a dull, torpid existence, in the mere enjoyments of sense, till suddenly a wave of thought seems to pervade the mass, the Promethean fire is lighted afresh, the spirit with which the atmosphere is charged fills every bosom, and the spark soon kindles into a glowing flame.

These are the epochs when great events take place, when thrones are demolished, kingdoms are set up or cast down, ancient fetters broken, and great reforms accomplished. A period of rest then again ensues, the people take to the new state of things, and those who are in comfortable circumstances fondly hope that all things will endure for ever. But this can never be; in the affairs of mankind striving towards perfection, the eternal law of nature rules that ebb and flow shall continually succeed each other, and that, after each period of stagnation, a fresh impulse shall set all again in motion, so that a new and improved state of things may rise from the ruins of old and obsolete institutions. The middle of the eighteenth century was marked by one of these great epochs.

\ The state of Germany in the first half of the

eighteenth century has been described by native historians as a deplorable example of decay, serfdom, and debasement; between the privileged classes and the working multitude the chasm was so immeasurable, that there was indeed nothing in common among them but the air they breathed. All feeling of nationality was extinct, public opinion was tyrannically suppressed, the nobles were depraved, and the citizens callous. With regard to the lower classes—the peasants, they were the poorest of the poor, from whom soldiers were enlisted by means of a mixture of fraud and force; unmanned by a boundless oppression, they were regarded as something beyond the pale of humanity. Even in the year 1750, expressions were made use of in public edicts with reference to the lower classes, which educated persons of the present day would hesitate to employ when speaking of the very beasts of the field. The so-called abodes of learning partook of the general wretched and barbarous state of society, inasmuch as we find that the teachers in the German Universities vied with the students in swaggering, duelling, intoxication, and other disgraceful excesses. Ignorance, neglect, and vulgarity characterised the lecture-room, the pulpit, and the public offices. The jurisprudence was worthy of the prevailing theology, evidenced by the monstrous atrocity of the penal code. So recently as 1749, a poor old man was burnt alive for sorcery at Wartzburg.

Such was the state of the people in Prussia, that when Frederick the Great ascended the throne in 1740, he expressed his opinion that the people were fit for nothing but to eat, drink, and fight. The opinions of that great monarch are fully expressed in a letter to Voltaire, from his camp in 1741, the substance of which is as follows:—

" Religion, the ancient idol which credulous men venerate, is sustained solely by prejudice, caprice, and ignorance. Truth fulminated against the monster in Greece, and Lucretius, by his talented writing, attacked it at Rome. You also have used your efforts to render man incredulous by removing the veil from that silly dream which has ruled for so long a time; but man, weak and stupid man, still clings to his old superstition. Believe me it is a waste of labour to employ sound sense, and use arguments to beasts of burden who drag the plough. When the war is over come to Berlin, and let us, Epicurus-like, enjoy the present life and the goods of this world. . . . . Men are not fit to receive the truth. I look upon them as a mere herd of deer in the park of a great lord; their only function is to people and fill up the enclosure."

When we reflect on the state of Germany in general and Prussia in particular at that time, it really seems as if Frederick was not far wrong; his father had drilled his subjects into a mere herd of animals; all their feelings and noble aspirations rigorously nipped in the bud; the very idea of freedom thoroughly rooted out of their hearts by an irresponsible despotism; how was it possible that Frederick should find himself at the head of anything but a nation of slaves?

It might have been well for his country if Frederick had paid attention to that which Voltaire pointed out to him in his answer to the above letter which we have quoted. "I fear your Majesty will get to despise mankind too much." But the King had formed his opinion, and did not believe that his subjects were capable of improvement. This was his error, and the result of it was shown when his system broke down, and fell before the energy of a people who had inscribed liberty and the rights of man on its banners.

Prussia had inherited a simple despotism from Frederick the Great; all independent spirit had been effectually stamped out of the nation; the isolation of classes was complete, and all the higher offices—civil and military—were declared to be the inalienable right of the nobles.

The army, officered entirely from the nobility, made themselves conspicuous by a brutal contempt for the whole burgher class, and had no sympathy with the people. This evil was rendered much more oppressive under the infamous government of Frederick II.; for, although Frederick the Great was essentially a despot, still he was a conscientious and able one, who used his power for the good of the State; while Frederick II., a slave to sensuality, took little heed of state affairs, which were managed by an incompetent bureaucracy. If we add to this that the feudal laws were in full vigour, and the land in the possession of large proprietors to whom the peasants were vassals, we may form some idea of the miserable state of servitude of the Prussian nation when Frederick William III. came to the throne.

Frederick William III. although a good man who wished to rule well, was essentially a weak prince. Infirm of purpose and diffident of his own judgment, he had inherited most of the prejudices of his race, and hated the idea of any change. Like all weak men, he was ruled by his subordinates; and these—such as Luchesini, Lombard, &c.—were of the lowest sensual grade, and in their characters the immorality prevalent in the court of Frederick II. was fully exemplified; without principle, firmness, or patriotism, they were the very worst kind of men to be at the helm during the storm which was about to break over the Prussian nation.

Heinrich Frederic Karl, Baron von Stein, was born in Nassau in 1757. He was the youngest of four sons, and the ninth of ten children. His family belonged to the old nobility of Western Germany. The family estate was small, and had been for a lengthened period much involved. His father, Karl Philipp von Stein, was a type of the old German barons, brave and honourable, mediocre in intellect, and whose chief occupation was the chase. His mother was a very superior person, and appears to have exercised a lasting influence on her son.

She is described as being most conscientious in the discharge of her duties, of great firmness and determination in the ordering of her household; clear in her judgment; but of a somewhat hasty, and at times violent, temper, which was, however, softened by her strong religious feeling.

Stein, from an early period, was destined for a political career, and he applied himself with great diligence to his studies from his youth up. History, especially English history, was his favourite study. At the age of sixteen he was sent to the world-renowned University of Göttingen, where he remained four years, and when his studies were completed in 1777, he travelled and visited different courts in Germany, and thus made himself acquainted with the more important political questions of the day.

It was during these travels, from 1777—1780, that Stein became aware of the rottenness of the whole German administration, and had a presentiment of its speedy dissolution.

In his twenty-seventh year, Frederick the

Great employed him on a diplomatic mission, which he skilfully conducted; in 1786 he was created a privy councillor, and paid a visit to England, where he remained nine months, returning much impressed, and with a hearty admiration of the political, social, and industrial relations of the country. In 1787 he refused the post of ambassador to the Hague and St. Petersburg, notwithstanding the splendour of such a position, which would have tempted most men, for he felt that his usefulness lay in Germany, in his Fatherland; and as duty was always the first consideration before which all personal or selfish views were bound to succumb, he never hesitated for a moment in his decision.

Towards the end of 1792 the consequences of the great French Revolution, and the coalition which was directed against it, occupied the attention of Stein. He had little sympathy with the Revolution even at first, before its destructive energies had been developed. |His leaning was essentially aristocratic, and his ideas of freedom did not square with the enthusiastic theories of Rousseau, and still less with those of Voltaire. Philosophic and impracticable ideas of equality and fraternity, as well as the French scheme of the universal rights of man, clashed with his political and private views. He considered that different degrees and classes of society were necessary for its natural and proper constitution. The complete annihilation of the class privileges of the nobility and clergy seemed to him a monstrous error, however zealous he may have been afterwards in abolishing those which he considered obsolete and unjust. The shameful humiliation and abolition of Royalty, coupled with the bloodthirsty rule of the Republic which quickly followed, made Stein one of the most decided opponents of the Revolution. That he thought so little of the energy and duration of the " abominable French nation" is a strong proof of the fact that the most able men are frequently among the most shortsighted in human affairs.

It is to be presumed that the sudden and unexpected advance of the French legions under Custine, and the fall of Mainz, which opened the way for the stranger into the heart of Germany must have considerably shaken him in his views. His brother, Colonel Stein, had foreseen the danger months previously, and had lamented the folly and ignorance of the Government in leaving a place of such consequence undefended.

Stein made himself very active in the service of his country: he became President of the Upper House, and on the death of Struensee was appointed Finance Minister 27 Oct. 1804.

As the chief object of this small brochure is to give a brief popular account of the Reforms of Stein with regard to the Land, we shall not follow the course of events in Europe during the next few years, which, indeed, are sufficiently well known; enough for our purpose is the fact, that Prussia's humiliation commenced on the fatal field of Jena, 14 Oct. 1806. The news of the unfortunate battle was imparted to the citizens of Berlin on the 17 Oct. by Count

Schulenburg in the now historical words—" The King has lost a battle. Calm is now the first duty of a citizen. I request this of you."

Having issued this important recommendation, the very next day this noble Governor deserted his post and fled, without having made the slightest effort towards the defence of the city. It is a remarkable fact that the citizens of Berlin not only followed out the above advice to the letter, but in many instances greeted the entry of the French Emperor with cries of " Vive l'Empereur." Such was the state of servility into which the Prussian people had been drilled by the tyranny of the aristocracy, that the French were in a great measure looked upon as deliverers by the town population, who regarded the defeat which their army had sustained as a just chastisement of the arrogance of the nobles and a righteous judgment on the officer caste.

Stein, exasperated at the vacillation of the King, who still wished to retain his old ministers, positively refused to enter into the Cabinet with-

out Hardenberg, or with Beyme. The King hesitated for a time, but at length on the 3rd January, 1807, he brought things to a crisis in a violent autograph letter to Stein which concluded with the following words:—
"From all this, I have observed with the greatest sorrow that I have not been mistaken in you from the beginning, and that you are to be regarded as a perverse, refractory, obstinate, and disobedient servant of the State, who, vain of his own talents and far from having the good of the State in view, is merely led by caprice, and acts only from passion, personal hatred and bitterness. Such officials are exactly those whose mode of proceeding is the most disadvantageous and dangerous for the maintenance of the State. It pains me truly that you have rendered it necessary for me to speak in such plain language to you. However, as you give yourself out to be a lover of truth, I have given you my opinion in plain German, and I feel myself called upon to add, that if you do not choose to correct your

disrespectful and offensive behaviour, the State cannot reckon much on you for further service."

Stein was lying on a sick bed when he received this letter. He immediately replied, " Since your Majesty looks upon me as a 'perverse, refractory, obstinate and disobedient servant of the State, who, vain of his own talents and far from having the good of the State in view is merely led by caprice, and acts only from passion, personal hatred and bitterness,' and as I also am fully convinced that ' such officials are exactly those whose operation is most disadvantageous and dangerous for the maintenance of the State,' I must request your Majesty to accept my resignation."

On the 4th January, the King answered him, " Since the Baron von Stein has pronounced his own sentence under yesterday's date I have nothing more to add." Thus Stein saw that he was dismissed, although he never received any official document to that effect.

In this manner, a most efficient public servant,

the man of the greatest capacity in the whole State, was lost to Prussia at the very moment when he might have proved a prop to the falling edifice, which received its last blow on the raft at Tilsit on the 9th July, 1807, when the humiliating peace was concluded by which Prussia was robbed of all her lands beyond the Elbe on the west, together with Magdeburg and all her Polish possessions on the east. Prussia thus lost 2983 square (German) miles of territory, with 4,476,000 inhabitants—more than the half of her possessions, as she retained only a space of 2173 square miles, with 5,707,000 inhabitants; besides this, she remained disarmed and subject to the arbitrary will of Napoleon.

Thus the proud State of Frederick the Great was partitioned and trodden under foot, and the diadem of the Hohenzollerns lay shattered at the feet of a soldier of fortune. The King, indeed, bore his fate with great equanimity and dignity, but he stood alone, helpless, and without advisers, deserted by all who could afford him aid and support towards re-establishing his affairs, for Napoleon had insisted on the dismissal of Hardenberg as the first condition of peace. Bitterly indeed must the King have repented his foolish conduct in dismissing Stein,—now the only man in his dominions who was capable of raising the country from its ashes. Fortunately, that good man never allowed his private injuries to interfere with the duty he owed to his fatherland. He had retired to his estate in Nassau, but his great merit and capacity did not escape the acute observation of the Emperor of Russia, who offered him the place of Count Romanzow, who was retiring from the post of Minister of the Russian Board of Trade. Stein would have accepted this offer under certain conditions, but the negociation finally fell through on account of the war and other political reasons. In the meantime Hardenberg used all his influence with the King to get Stein reinstated in his position, and we find that during the leisure of his retirement he occupied himself in drawing up a plan for the thorough reorganization of the Prussian administration, and a great general reform in her social relations. One of the principal points of which was—

The creation of a free peasant class, by means of the emancipation of the land and soil.

Stein's recall and reinstatement was decided on as soon as Hardenberg's dismissal had become inevitable. Napoleon, as well as the Emperor of Russia, pointed out Stein as the only statesman on whom the King of Prussia could still rely; but he, who was then at the summit of his power, could not foresee that he was preparing a post for his most dangerous and irreconcilable enemy, to whose influence his later fall may be ascribed. At this time a pressing letter from Hardenberg set before Stein the strong desire of the King to place him at the head of the German government. The letter described the desperate condition of the State and of the King, and dwelt upon his dignified conduct in misfortune, pointing out to him that it was his sacred duty to forget the injuries that he had suffered, and to place all personal considerations in the background when the fate of the kingdom was at stake. Still more pressingly and affectionately wrote to him the Princess Louisa von Radzowil, sister of Prince Louis, who was killed in the war. The affecting description of the situation and the patience of the King; the reliance on Stein's noble sense of self-sacrifice, as well as of his talent and power to save the State, must have made a profound impression on him. He did not hesitate one moment in his decision; without any reflection on the past, or asking any conditions or guarantees for the future, he at once acceded to the invitation of his King, his Fatherland, and his duty. His answer to the King was conceived as follows:—" The gracious commands of your Majesty, which invite me again to undertake the ministry of home affairs, have been received by me through the Cabinet Minister Hardenberg, dated Munich, the 10th of July, on the 9th of August. I accept the appointment at once, unconditionally, and I leave to your Majesty the decision of every relation, whether of business or of persons with whom it may seem good to your Majesty that I should work. At this time of universal misfortune, it would show a great want of moral courage were I to allow any personal feeling to prevent my coming again into office, and so much the more as your Majesty himself has given so distinguished an example of constancy."

Such is the record of Stein's true nobility of soul, and perhaps in the whole history of statesmanship there is no other example of a statesman having performed so much in so short a time as Stein, while he was Prussian Minister from the 30th September 1807, to the 24th of November, 1808.

Thus recalled, and placed at the head of affairs, Stein at once proceeded zealously to organize a reform of the internal political affairs of the State. He was convinced that his countrymen were capable of rising from the depths of degradation into which they had sunk, and that it was in his power to accomplish a national regeneration, and place Germany as a centre of European civilization; in short, he believed in himself and in the power of his will to accomplish this task. The chief point of the programme which he laid before the King, with regard to the internal administration, may be thus briefly stated :—

"That which the State has lost in extent must be made up for by unremitted and increased energy. The old state of affairs has past away; all must be reconstructed if Prussia is to rise from her ruins, and again assume her place among the states of Europe. Among the remnants of the former great powers of the State there are hostile elements; these must be eliminated, in order to make a compact unity. The different classes of the nation are in direct opposition, because one is favoured to the detriment of the other. Union affords strength: if this is to be secured, equal rights must be enjoyed by all classes alike.

"The duties to the State appertain to all inhabitants in an equal degree. Every individual should be personally free and acknowledge no master except the King, governing according to law; there should be a national representation in parliament. No one in the State, whether individual or corporative, ought to be allowed to be judge in his own cause. Education ennobles a people, and according to its degree, so does a country take its place and rank among civilized nations; it is the true condition of all profitable progress and order, of all power and prosperity. The State must promote it. The land and soil of the country must be accessible to all purchasers alike. *The possession and acquirement of the land by the people, must be facilitated by stringent legislative measures.*

Such were the measures recommended by Stein. They speak for themselves; we, however, shall only go into the history of the last mentioned point.

Emancipation of the Peasant Class.

Law 9— 28 Oct. 1807.

Stein's object in the first place, as soon as he found that he had the power, was to re-construct the State from the foundations.

More than three-fourths of the whole population were not in the enjoyment of personal liberty, inasmuch as they were serfs to the great landed proprietors, and the land which they tilled, and on which their maintenance depended, was not at their own disposal. They had the use of it indeed, under certain conditions, but this was not sufficient; a free class of peasant proprietors was the desideratum, to which the efforts of legislation were to be directed if any permanent national benefit was to result.

It would be foreign to our purpose here to enter into minute details, regarding the different forms of villeinage which existed at this time in Prussia, by making distinctions between those peasants in whose bodies the lord had a right of property, and those who were subject to the manor by inheritance, or who were what is called "adscripti glebæ;" sufficient is it to say that the lowest kinds of villeins were entirely subject to their masters; at their death, the bulk of any property they may have had went to their lord; their children could not marry without his consent, and were generally kept as servants without any remuneration save food; corporal punishment was also allowed, though not extending to life.

The greater part of the peasants, however, were above this lower kind, and had certain fixed dues to render, and had the power of purchasing their freedom at a fixed price.

The free peasant paid no dues in person, and he held a kind of lease, in which there were conditions. He could not purchase other peasants' land, or practise any trade or profession except agriculture.

Upon the whole, the status of the peasant in

Prussia when Stein undertook his reforms, was very similar to that of the English peasant at the commencement of the sixteenth century, to which circumstance we shall have occasion to refer hereafter.

The following are the principal points of the edict of the 9th October, which, translated into English, is taken from an essay published by the Cobden Club.

"We, Frederick William, by the Grace of God, &c., &c. Be it known unto all men that :—

"Whereas, owing to the universal character of the prevailing misery, it would surpass our means to relieve each person individually, and, even if we could, the objects we have at heart would not be fulfilled" (loquitur, the mediæval father of his people) :—

"And, whereas it is not only conformable to the everlasting dictates of justice, but likewise to the principles of a sound national economy, to remove all hindrances in the way of the individual attaining to that measure of material well-being which his capacities may enable him to attain" (loquitur, Adam Smith):—

"And whereas the existing restrictions, partly on the possession and enjoyment of landed property, partly in connexion with the personal condition of the agricultural population, obstruct in an especial manner our benevolent intentions, and exercise a baleful influence, the one by diminishing the value of land and impairing the credit of the landed proprietor, the other by diminishing the value of labour: we are minded that both should be restrained within the limits which the public welfare requires, and therefore we decree and ordain as follows:—

"*Abolition of Villeinage.*

"§ 10. From the day of the publication of this edict no new relations of villeinage, either by birth, marriage, or acquisition of a villein-holding can be created.

"§ 11. From the same date, all peasants holding by hereditary tenures, cease, they and their wives and their children, to be villeins.

"§ 12. From Martinmas 1810, every remaining form of villeinage in all our dominions shall cease, and from that date there shall be none but freemen in our dominions. It is to be understood, however, that these freemen remain subject to all obligations flowing from the possession of land, or from particular contracts to which, as freemen, they can be subjected.

"*Free Exchange of Real Property.*

"§ 1. Every inhabitant of our dominions, as far as the State is concerned, is henceforth free to acquire and own landed property of every kind and description. The noble, therefore, can acquire not only noble land, but burgher and peasant land, so also the burgher and the peasant can acquire not only burgher and peasant land, *i.e.*, land not noble, but likewise noble land. Every such transfer of real estate must, however, continue, as before, to be notified to the authorities.

"*Freedom in regard to Choice of Occupation.*

"§ 2. Every noble, without derogation to his rank, is henceforth free to exercise the trades and callings of the burgher—the burgher may become peasant, the peasant burgher.

"*In how far Rights of Pre-emption still exist.*

"§ 3. (This paragraph is technical, and does not alter the principle of the measure.)

"*Division of Property.*

"§ 4. All owners of real property, in its nature saleable, can after due notice to the provincial authority, sell the same piecemeal and in detail as well as in block. Co-proprietors can in the same way divide amongst them property owned in common.

"*Free power of Granting Leases.*

"§ 5. Every proprietor, whether or not his

property forms part of a fief or of any other kind of entailed property, is free to grant leases of any duration, so long as the moneys received in payment of such leaseholds are used to pay off mortgages, and in the case of an entailed property, are capitalized for the benefit of the estate.

"*Extinction and Consolidation of Peasant Holdings.*

"§ 6. When a landed proprietor is of opinion that he cannot restore to their former condition or keep up the several peasant establishments on his property, he may, if the holdings have not got the character of hereditary tenures (*i.e., Anglicè*, if they are not of the nature of copyhold or perpetual leaseholds), after the particular case has been inquired into by the Government of the province, and with the sanction of that Government, consolidate such holdings into one large peasant holding, or incorporate them with demesne land.

"Special instructions as to the cases in which

this process shall be permitted will be sent to the provincial Governments.

"§ 7. If, on the other hand, the tenures are of a hereditary kind, no change whatever can be effected without the previous acquisition by purchase, or in some other legal manner, of the rights of the actual possessors. Such cases likewise require the formalities specified in § 6 (*i.e.*, *the previous sanction of the Government*).

"Facilities for Mortgaging Entailed Estates to pay Losses occasioned by War.

"§ 8. (The provisions of this paragraph are of a temporary kind.)

" *Of the cutting off of Entails.*

"§ 9. Every entailed estate, whatever the nature of that entail, can be freed from the entail by the consent of the family."

Thus the greater part of the population was freed from servitude, and converted into a great free peasant class, by which, for the first time, the body of the people obtained an interest in the State. The productive power of the land was also greatly increased by its being freed from restrictions, and the consciousness among the people of possessing a free right of property, created at once a new and active power within the nation.

By this edict also the partition walls of class privilege were broken through, and the free traffic in, and power of partitioning, land put an end to the obstructive permanency which had hitherto been the rule, and gave a due opportunity to talent and capital to exercise their legitimate rights and privileges.

But notwithstanding this decree, the peasant was not wholly master of the soil he cultivated : the proper direction however had been clearly pointed out, and the way was plainly indicated to further consequences. It was very apparent that this decree was only the forerunner of further legislation, which however did not take place till four years afterwards.

At this time it may be well imagined that Stein had made many enemies. The French authorities were watching his proceedings, and they soon saw that their interests would be seriously affected. The "Junkerpartei," as the Prussian nobility were called, hated him cordially, and only waited an opportunity for active opposition. To their shame be it said, they called themselves "the Peace party," the party of the French, and did not hesitate to prefer what they considered their private interests to those of their country. A German historian remarks,— "Too selfish to sacrifice their privileges for the good of the Fatherland, too cowardly openly to oppose the popular measures, they did not hesitate to take shelter under the wing of a foreign despot, and surrender the independence of their country rather than their own privileges." Peace and the French alliance was their battle-cry; their secret object to overthrow Stein and his reforms. The emancipation of the peasants, the abolition of class privileges in civil and military affairs, was gall and wormwood to them. The King, however, although a weak man, was not a wicked one, and he had sufficient penetration to see through the artifices of Stein's adversaries, whose representations concerning the evil tendency of the new measures were supported by men of the highest rank and position, and, we regret to say, also by many moving in the learned circles of Berlin, who concealed their secret egotism under the mask of an outward show of patriotism. This ignoble crew pushed their enmity so far as to enlist Napoleon on their side. For the time, however, all their efforts failed, and Stein continued his endeavours to strengthen the force of the nation, hoping thereby to free it from the oppressive tyranny of the French incubus. In a remarkable memorial which at this time, early in August, 1807, Stein laid before the King, the following noble passage occurs :—

"It should seriously be considered that the power to be assailed is great, and the spirit which conducts it a mighty one. The struggle once commenced will be undertaken, less in view of a probability of success than from a certainty that, without it, there can be no solution of the difficulty, and that it would be more in accordance with the duty we owe to our contemporaries and posterity, more glorious for the King and nation to succumb sword in hand than to remain continually chained in captivity. To follow out the path which we propose to tread, we must make ourselves familiar with privations of every kind, as well as with death. If we have made this essential resolution and preparation, let us commence, in God's name, when favourable circumstances offer ; and above all, let us not forget that, by courage and intrepidity, great results may be obtained with very small means. But for this end, all those inert, wretched beings whose sense for all noble feeling is so blunted as to make them incapable of any devotion or self-sacrifice, must be dismissed : such wretches only paralyze and destroy all that they come in contact with; peaceful enjoyment being the sole object of their mean and pitiful natures."

Again, on the 11th August, Stein wrote to the King:—

"No ruler can be doubtful for a moment concerning the question whether it is better tamely and patiently to await the sentence of an infamous tyrant, or to renew the sanguinary struggle for honour, independence, and the throne."

Here it may be instructive as well as amusing to examine the arguments used to combat Stein's reforms, which we think will plainly show how prejudice and self-interest, real or fancied, can blind the mind and pervert the judgment even of otherwise highly gifted men. Field-Marshal Count York von Wartenburg, who played one of the most conspicuous parts in the war of deliverance, has left the following on record, and the document is all the more valuable from the fact that some of his objections to Stein's plan for placing the peasant firmly on the soil are being urged at the present day in England against a similar proceeding which is in progress, prompted by similar motives.

"The man (Stein), to our misfortune, has been in England, and it is from thence that he has imbibed his ideas of statesmanship, and now he thinks to apply the institutions of a country which are founded on centuries of naval superiority, commerce and manufactures, to our poor clod-breaking Prussia. No sooner does he make his appearance at Memel than out comes an edict that every citizen, without distinction, shall be permitted to purchase a manor, and that noblemen may be permitted to exercise a trade or profession at their own discretion! Why, such a humiliation, or I may say, insult to the nobility, is utterly against the feelings both of the King and of the people of Prussia. Will the greengrocer, I ask, or the tailor, or the speculator who may acquire a property, and who would only look upon it as a mercantile transaction, be fit persons to serve their King in misfortune, and will they be inclined to risk life and property for his sake? Will the peasants on such a manor evince the attachment to such parvenu masters as they have been wont to do to the ancient hereditary possessors? They may, indeed, welcome such masters with triumphal arches, amid ill-suppressed laughter and ridicule, but such parvenus never can have the same influence over the minds of their dependents, neither will they command the same love and respect.

"Another thing: this talk about the so-called slavery of the peasant; what is it but mere philanthropic clap-trap, as all men know right well, also their assumption that an estate should be like a dollar in money, which multiplies itself by circulation; but then through the stamp dues, the State would be a loser. This is certainly not in accordance with the old national paternal views of the King, but must rather have been hatched in the counting-house of some banker or learned professor, who comes forth preaching a very ill-digested sermon from Adam Smith.

Unfortunately our talented minister is under the thumb of rabble of this kind (*geschmeiss*). Do we not see what things come to light out of his coterie? Why, do we not hear the democratic absurdity that all places in the State are to be filled according to the votes of the people? Only conceive how our beautiful country will be cut up by this scheming system! The King's domains too are to be alienated, no exception is to be made even with regard to these, and so the King is to be made a mere pensioner. The speculator who acquires a property will only think of the present, and will proceed to cut down the splendid oak and beech forests because they do not pay so well as arable land; the old ancestral trees will be seen no more, and birch and American poplars will take their place as being quicker in growth.

"Another hobby which this minister rides is the population: from the family of every honest citizen and mechanic who employs and maintains a number of workmen a swarm of small families will crop up, every clodhopper will marry his wench and beget a fresh race of famishing paupers. And the land too, if they have their way, will be cut up into small holdings, every inheritance will be divided; and thus, instead of a prosperous noble possessor, or a proprietor of half a hide of land, we shall have a swarm of gardeners or cottage proprietors at the best; and when all the large villages are replaced by hamlets, and the free landed proprietor fences in his couple of acres with a hedge and takes up his fowling-piece to go shooting on his estate—then, I say, we shall witness the beau ideal at which they are driving. Yes, indeed, the population will most certainly increase—the calculation is just; but would not such a population (and we may thank God that we have not yet got one like that of England or France) resemble the vermin begotten in old wood shavings?

"Then again, this violent abolition of the feudal service of the peasants, without any compensation to the proprietor! What division will it not create among classes, and thus play the game of the enemy. But it never can be carried into execution literally; without modification it would be a direct attack on the rights of property. Frederick William will hardly be willing to blot out the fundamental principle of Prussia, *suum cuique*,* from the star of his Order and substitute that of St. Crispin in its place. For the rest, the views of the minister are well known: he wishes to show the peasant an El Dorado looming in the distance; to enjoy it he has nothing to do but chase the French out of the land. This is the aim of all the secret societies in Germany, which Napoleon has already smelt out, and for which we owe him no reproach if the King should not be compromised in them. *The person of the monarch and the security of his house should always be placed above all other considerations by a Prussian Minister of State.*"

---

* *Suum cuique*—i.e., give to every man his own. St. Crispin was the patron of thieves.

STEIN AND HIS REFORMS.

Such were the arguments used by a German Tory in the year 1807: we shall have occasion to refer to them hereafter when we are considering the Tory arguments against a land reform which are used in England at the present day. Human nature seems never essentially to change: the language of prejudice and selfishness always takes the same tone of bitterness whenever opposition is made to unjust claims and pretensions.

The efforts of Stein to effect a general rising in order to shake off the foreign yoke, and his constant memorials to the King urging him to give his consent to his projects, which were never relaxed for a moment, excited the jealousy of the Tory French party, who did all in their power to work his ruin. For this purpose they did not scruple to enlist Napoleon on their side, so that it is hardly to be wondered at, that Stein's fall was at hand. On the 24th November, 1808, on its being represented to the King that so long as Stein remained in office it was impossible to expect anything from the good offices of Napoleon,

Stein's dismissal was signed. The King knew his worth, and expressed to him in the letter of dismissal, " how painful it was to him to find himself compelled to part with a man of his character, who had the most just claims to his confidence and that of the nation."

Thus ended the one year's tenure of Stein's ministry. After his dismissal he went first to Berlin with the intention of proceeding from thence to Breslau, there to await events and a favourable opportunity of again making himself useful to his country. At the beginning of January, however, the French ambassador, St. Marsan, arrived in Berlin, bringing with him the following declaration of Napoleon against Stein:—

" One Stein (le nommé Stein) having sought to raise disturbances in Germany, is declared an enemy of France and the Rhenish Confederation.

" The property which the aforesaid Stein may possess, whether in France or in the Rhenish Confederacy, will be sequestrated.

"The said Stein will be arrested in his person wherever he may be found by our, or the Confederate, troops.

"Given under our hand in the Imperial Court of Madrid, Dec. 16th, 1808.

(Signed) "NAPOLEON."

Let us pause here for one moment to reflect on this infamous and tyrannical proceeding. To what humiliating depths of debasement must Prussia have sunk when her King was obliged to acquiesce against his will in such a deplorable abuse of power! Here was a French monarch, passing judgment, without any trial, on the subject and Prime Minister of an independent German Prince, seizing arbitrarily on his property, and compelling the whole of the German Princes of the Rhenish Confederation to carry out his iniquitous decree. It was the old story, *væ victis!* How profound the feeling of humiliation, how bitter must have been the cup to the King, when he saw his Prime Minister—

perhaps the only man in his dominions to whom the nation had to look for the regeneration of the country—condemned without a hearing, and banished as though he had been a common malefactor.

Stein bowed to the inevitable, and secretly left Berlin, January 6th, 1809, not, however, without the privity of the French ambassador. He passed the frontier into Austria, on the 12th of January, with a heavy heart, and four years were destined to pass before he was again enabled to return to his country under very different circumstances.

The next step with regard to the land reform occurred under the ministry of Hardenberg. The following is a translation of the legislation for that purpose, on Sep. 14th, 1811, which we extract from the essays of the Cobden Club :—

Legislation with Regard to the Land Question,

September 14th, 1811.

The edict of 1807, great and incisive as had been its operation, was of a negative kind. It removed disabilities, undid the shackles which bound the peasant to the glebe, allowed such rights as existed to be used freely, and pulled down the walls which separated from each other the different classes of society. But it created no new forms of property: it proclaimed freedom of exchange, but it did not provide the title-deeds required as the first condition of exchange. Peasants' land could now be held indiscriminately by all the citizens of the State, but it was still held under the old forms of tenure; there were still two dominia. The lord was still owner of the peasants' land, but had no right to its possession. The peasant was in a measure free, but was not master of his labour.

The legislation of 1811 stepped in to remedy

this state of things, and applying to the monarchy generally the principles which during the last three years had proved in the highest degree successful when applied to the State domains, it set itself to substitute allodial ownership for feudal tenure.

Its work was in the highest degree positive.

The legislation of 1811 mainly consists of two great edicts, both bearing the same date, that of the 14th of September. The one entitled, "Edict for the Regulation of the Relations between the Lords of the Manor and their Peasants." The other, "Edict for the better Cultivation of the Land."

The first is concerned with the creation of new title-deeds for the peasant holders, and with the commutation of the services rendered in virtue of the old title-deeds.

The second surveys the whole field of agrarian reform, and introduces general measures of amelioration.

The preamble to the "Edict for the Regulation of the Relations between Landlord and Tenant" recites how "We, Frederick William, by the grace of God King of Prussia, having convinced ourselves, both by personal experience in our own domains, and by that of many lords of manors, of the great advantages which have accrued both to the lord and to the peasant by the transformation of peasant holdings into property, and the commutation of the services and dues on the basis of a fair indemnity, and having consulted, in regard to this weighty matter, experienced farmers, and skilled persons of all kinds belonging to all our provinces, and to all ranks of our subjects, ordain and decree as follows:"—

The edict then branches off into two main parts.

The first dealing with peasant holdings in which the tenant has hereditary rights; the second with holdings in which the tenant has no hereditary rights.

Part I.

All tenants of hereditary holdings (*i.e.*, holdings which are inherited according to the common law, or in which the lord of the manor is bound to select as tenant one or other of the heirs of the last tenant), *whatever the size of the holding*, shall by the present edict become the proprietors of their holdings, after paying to the landlord the indemnity fixed by this edict.

On the other hand, all claims of the peasant on the manor, for the keeping in repair of his farm buildings, &c., shall cease.

We desire that landlords and tenants should of themselves come to terms of agreement, and give them two years from the date of this edict to do so. If within that time the work is not done, the State will undertake it.

The rights to be commuted may be thus generally classed :—

I. Rights of the landlord.

   1. Right of ownership (" dominium directum ").

2. Claim to services.
3. Dues in money and kind.
4. Dead stock of the farms.
5. Easements, or servitudes on the land held.

II. Rights of the tenant.
1. Claim to assistance in case of misfortune.
2. Right to gather wood, and other forest rights, in the forest of the manor.
3. Claim upon the landlord, for repairs of buildings.
4. Claim upon the landlord, in case tenant is unable to pay public taxes.
5. Pasturage rights on demesne lands or forests.

Of these different rights only a few—viz., the dues paid in kind or money, the dead stock, and the servitudes, are capable of exact valuation.

The others can only be approximately estimated.

To obtain, therefore, a solid foundation for the work of commutation, and not to render it nugatory by difficulties impossible to be overcome, we deem it necessary to lay down certain rules for arriving at this estimate, and to deduce those rules from the general principles laid down by the laws of the State.

These principles are:—

1. That in the case of hereditary holdings, neither the services nor the dues can, under any circumstances, be raised.
2. That they must, on the contrary, be lowered if the holder cannot subsist at their actual rate.
3. That the holding must be maintained in a condition which will enable it to pay its dues to the State.

From these three constitutional principles, as well as from the general principles of public law, it follows that the right of the State, both to ordinary and extraordinary taxes, takes precedence of every other right, and that the services to the manor are limited by the obligation which the latter is under to leave the tenant sufficient means to subsist and to pay taxes.

We consider that both these conditions are fulfilled when the sum total of the dues and services rendered to the manor do not exceed one-third of the total revenue derived by an hereditary tenant from his holding. Therefore, with the exceptions to be hereafter described, the rule shall obtain :

That, in the case of hereditary holdings, the lords of the manor shall be indemnified for their rights of ownership in the holding, and for the ordinary services and dues attached to the holding, when the tenants shall have surrendered one-third portion of all the lands held by them, and shall have renounced their claims to all extraordinary assistance, as well as to the dead stock, to repairs, and to the payment on their behalf of the dues to the State when incapable of doing so.

The edict then goes on to lay down the rules to be observed in applying this principle.

These rules presuppose the existence of the agricultural community referred to in the earlier part of this Paper—viz., equal allotments in an arable mark; the division of the arable mark in which these several allotments are situated into three "*Commonable Fields*" or "Fluren," a common system of cultivation obligatory on the community, in order to secure the community's right of pasture on the fallow and stubbles: and common rights of property in common lands occupied "de indiviso," mostly pasture lands, woods, &c., but sometimes also in arable common lands.

As a rule, the lord of the manor is to acquire possession of one of the three fields, or of one-third portion of each field, and of one-third portion of the common lands.

We have no space to enter into the details of the arrangements which provide for the cases differing from these.

As noted above, the lords and the peasants are left free to make what arrangements they please, as long as the proportion of one-third is maintained—*i.e.*, the indemnity may take the form of a payment of capital, or of a corn or money rent. Yet the rule to be followed (and a departure from this rule must have a distinct motive) is that the indemnity must be paid in land where the holdings are over fifty "morgen," * but in the shape of a corn rent where the holdings are under that size.

As a matter of practical convenience to both parties, the absolute separation of proprietary right suffers some few exceptions; the first and most important is, that the lord retains the right of pasturing the manorial sheep on two-thirds of the fallow and stubbles of the arable mark; the peasant also continues to enjoy the right of collecting as much firewood in the demesne as he requires for his personal use; for this right, and for the acquisition of his house and farm buildings as well as his garden-plot (his allotment in the

---

* The Prussian acre is about equal to two-thirds of an English acre—a hundred English acres being equal to 158½ Prussian acres.

mark of the township), he continues to render services to the lord of the manor at times (*e.g.*, harvest) when extra hands are wanted. These services are, however, restricted to a maximum of ten days of team-work, and ten days of hand labour for a team-peasant, and ten days man's work, and ten days woman's work for a hand-peasant.

Several paragraphs of the edict are taken up with provisions for so apportioning the burdens on the holdings that nothing shall prevent their dismemberment and being sold or exchanged in single parcels. Among these provisions is one preventing the peasant from mortgaging his estate above one-fourth of its value.

Where corn rents are not paid punctually, the lord of the manor can exact services instead.

Part II.

The class of holdings treated of in the second part are those held at will, or for a term of years or for life. In these cases, the landlord gets an indemnity of one-half of the holding under much the same conditions as in the case of the hereditary holdings. When the conditions differ, they do so in favour of the lord of the manor.

By the edict, of which the above are the main provisions, entirely new conditions of land occupation were inaugurated, and corresponding changes became necessary in the other branches of the agricultural system.

The "Edict for the better Cultivation of the Land," published on the same day, had these changes in view.

Fully to understand what these changes were, and what was the nature of the agricultural reforms to be introduced into Prussia, the picture of the peasant community as a microcosmic reproduction of the old community of the mark must be kept in mind. The peasant occupier's tenement is situated, apart from his land, in a village or township; his estate is made up of a number of single lots or parcels (Grundstücke) distributed over the three main divisions or *Fields* (Fluren, Campi) into which the arable mark is divided. Often intermixed with these peasant parcels, and subject to the same obligatory cultivation, are parcels of demesne lands. In addition to his individual rights of possession in the arable mark, controlled by the common rights of pasturage on the stubbles, he has common rights in the common pasture, which common rights he shares with the lord of the manor. Besides these rights, he has rights of pasture, &c., in the forest lands of the demesne proper. The sum total of these individual and common rights makes up the peasant holding, correlative to which are the services to be rendered to the manor. As long as these services were calculated on the sum total of the rights enjoyed by the tenant, it was of paramount importance that no dismemberment should take place. Consequently, even in the case of freeholders, none but exceptional dismemberments were allowed.

Apart then from the relations between landlord

and tenant, or rather inseparably implicated in those relations, and therefore requiring simultaneous regulation, are the *common rights* of the peasants themselves, and the impediments which these common rights throw in the way of individual cultivation, and the free use of the rights of property about to be granted.

The ruling idea of the " Edict for the better Cultivation of the Land," as of its predecessor, and indeed of the whole legislation connected with the names of Stein and Hardenberg, is to enfranchise not the owner of land merely, but likewise the land owned by him, and to remove every obstacle which prevents the soil finding its way out of hands less able to cultivate it into those more competent to do so. Conformably to these principles, the edict in question, in the first place, removes all restrictions still existing in the way of free exchange in land, in so far as private rights (viz., rights arising from entails, servitudes, &c.) are not affected. By this proviso, the restrictions contained in paragraphs

6 and 7 of the Edict of 1807 were removed, the difference between tenant's land and demesne land ceased, and the lord of the manor could freely acquire the former without the previous sanction of the State. On the other hand, by the perfect liberty granted for dismemberment (the maxim being laid down that it was better, both for the cultivator and for the land cultivated, that the former should administer a small unencumbered estate rather than a large encumbered one), the advocates of the " petite culture " were conciliated. The passage in the edict is worth quoting *in extenso*, as it contains very explicitly what we have described as the ruling idea of the legislation we are discussing; an idea, it is true, which only attained its full development forty years later, but which nevertheless, in spite of the obstacles thrown in its way by the successors of Stein and Hardenberg, took sufficient root even at this early period to enable us to judge of its fruits. It is the idea of *ownership* versus *tenancy*, and of absolute freedom of

exchange and disposal; and special importance attaches to it as representing principles opposed both to the French system of compulsory division, and to the English system of tenancy, primogeniture, and strict settlement. The passage we refer to runs on as follows :—

"The proprietor shall henceforth (excepting always where the rights of third parties are concerned), be at liberty to increase his estate or diminish it, by buying or selling, as may seem good to him. He can leave the appurtenances thereof (the 'Grundstücke,' or parcels distributed in the three *Fields*) to one heir or to many, as he pleases. He may exchange them, or give them away, or dispose of them in any and every legal way, without requiring any authorization for such changes.

"This unlimited right of disposal has great and manifold advantages. It affords the safest and best means for preserving the proprietor from debt, and for keeping alive in him a lasting and lively interest in the improvement of his estate, and it raises the general standard of cultivation.

"The first of these results is obtained by the power it gives to the actual proprietor, or to an heir upon entering on his estate, to sell such portions as will enable him to provide for his heirs or co-heirs, as the case may be, or for any other extraordinary emergency, leaving what remains of the property unencumbered with mortgages or settlements.

"The interest in the estate is kept alive by the freedom left to parents to divide their estate amongst their children as they think fit, knowing that the benefit of every improvement will be reaped by them.

"Lastly, the higher standard of cultivation will be secured by land—which, in the hands of a proprietor without means, would necessarily deteriorate—getting into the hands of a proprietor with means, and therefore able to make the best of it. Without this power of selling portions of his property, the proprietor is apt to sink deeper and deeper into debt, and in proportion as he does so the soil is deprived of its strength. By selling, on the other hand, he becomes free from debt and free from care, and obtains the means of properly cultivating what remains to him. By this unhindered movement in the possession of land, the whole of the soil remains in a good state of cultivation; and this point once attained, increased industry and exertion will make it possible to attain a yet higher point, whereas a backward movement, except as the result of extraordinary mischances from without, is not to be apprehended.

"But there is yet another advantage springing from this power of piecemeal alienation which is well worthy of attention, and which fills our paternal heart with especial gladness. It gives, namely, an opportunity to the so-called small-folk (kleine Leute), cottiers, gardeners, boothmen, and day-labourers, to acquire landed property, and little by little to increase it. The prospect of such acquisition will render this numerous and useful class of our subjects industrious, orderly, and saving, inasmuch as thus only will they be enabled to obtain the means necessary to the purchase of land. Many of them will be able to work their way upwards, and to acquire property, and to make themselves remarkable for their industry. The State will acquire a new and valuable class of industrious proprietors; by the endeavour to become such, agriculture will obtain new hands, and by increased voluntary exertion more work out of the old ones."

The edict next enacts, as a supplementary measure to the " Edict for the Regulation of the Relations between Lords of the Manor," that in the case of hereditary leaseholds (Erbpächte) the services and fines may be commuted into rent-charges, and these rent-charges redeemed by a capital payment, calculated at four per cent.

It next proceeds to deal with the *common rights* of the peasants and of the lords; and here it fairly owns its inability to carry out the principle of the free owner on the free soil. The great mass of the peasant holdings are dispersed in small open "commonable" intermixed fields over the area of the arable mark; and the common rights of pasturage over the arable mark necessarily chain down the individual cultivator to the modes of cultivation compatible with these common rights. To disentangle this complicated web must be the work of time and of special legislation. The edict therefore announces a future law on the subject, and for the present confines itself to making provisions by which one-third part of such "commonable" fields can be freed from the common rights of pasturage, and placed at the absolute disposal of individual proprietors. The rights of pasturage in the forest lands of the manor are more easily disposed of; the advantageous terms on which full rights of property are obtainable by the peasants render it possible to make stringent regulations in regard to the exercise of those rights, in the interest of the landlord and for the preservation of the forests.

To guard against the possibility of a return to the double ownership system, the edict lays down the rule that, though a landed proprietor may settle labourers on his estate, and pay for their services in land, such contracts are never to be made for more than twelve years.

The edict concludes by expressing it to be his Majesty's wish and will that agricultural societies should be formed in every part of the country, for the purpose of collecting and diffusing knowledge. The expenses of these societies, and the salary of their secretaries, will be paid out of the Exchequer, and the societies themselves will be placed in communication with a central office in the capital, whose business it will also be to establish and maintain model farms in various parts of the country for the diffusion of agricultural knowledge. Besides this more or less unofficial machinery, provision is made for official agricultural boards to be established in each district; but these arrangements, having been superseded by subsequent legislation, need not be referred to.

The two edicts of the 14th September, 1811, may be considered as the culminating point of the legislation which goes by the name of Stein and Hardenberg.

Nothing could exceed the malicious joy of the aristocratic French party when Stein's dismissal, on the 24th November, appeared in the Gazette. Count York, whose characteristic letter we have already quoted, again committed his views to paper in a communication to Lieut.-Colonel von Oppen, and melancholy it is indeed that such a disgraceful record of narrow-mindedness and ignorance should have come down to us on the part of one who was otherwise a good man and an excellent officer.

" Our foreign relations begin to take a more favourable aspect; and our home affairs a more rational turn. One silly head has been already crushed; the other vile brood* will stifle in their own venom. I hope things will soon improve.

---

* Nattergeschmeiss—lit., excrement of vipers.

If calm reason holds sway as we hope, and fortune turns in our favour, I trust that the withered stem, animated afresh, will yet blossom and bear fruit."

We need not feel surprised at the narrow-minded and ignorant sentiments of a man of such a stamp as York. They are common to all countries alike. France had her Stein in Turgot some thirty years before this period, and he experienced the same fate.

We may be here pardoned a short digression in order, for the sake of comparison, to consider the preamble of the French edict for the emancipation of the peasant in 1776.

" Almighty God, in giving wants to mankind, in rendering necessary for him the resources of labour, has bestowed on every individual alike the right to labour as a property, and this property is the most sacred and absolute of all.

" We regard it as one of the first duties of our justice and an act the most worthy of our beneficence, to guard our subjects against all attacks on this inalienable right of man.

"It is our will therefore, to abolish all those institutions which prevent the indigent from living by his own labour, and which tend to depress a sex which, on account of its weakness, has more wants and less resources, and which seem, in condemning it to inevitable misery, to encourage seduction and vice;—which extinguish emulation and industry, and render useless the talents of those whose circumstances prevent them from entering into a corporation; which deprive the State and the Arts of all the enlightenment which may be brought to it by strangers; which retard the progress of these arts. . . .; and finally which, by the facility that they give to members of corporations to form leagues, to constrain the poorer classes to submit to the rule of the richer, become an instrument of monopoly, and favour manœuvres, the effect of which is to raise to an unnatural proportion the commodities most necessary for the subsistence of the people."

This was a direct attack on the privileged classes, who, putting themselves under the ægis of the principle of the rights of property which they declared to be violated by this edict, commenced an attack in which they found most zealous auxiliaries in all those who looked on a change in the law as a violation and suppression of all laws! Narrow-minded Conservatives! much more dangerous than the most dangerous innovators, whom we see at all epochs, who profane and imperil rights by defending, under that sacred name, the most intolerable abuses.

These Conservatives, however, triumphed for the time. Turgot's edict was reversed and he himself dismissed. The nobility, the parliament, the proprietors, all leagued against him, and though he bore his fall with equanimity it is said that he could not restrain his tears when he heard of the reversal of all his hopes. France was doomed to fifteen years more slavery, and then came the deluge when all privileges, all property was swept away, and centuries of tyranny and oppression ended in a sea of blood.

What a lesson to other nations. Had Turgot's reforms, and very moderate ones they were, been accepted, the French Revolution would never have occurred, for it would not have been necessary.

It is an error to maintain that this person or that caused the Revolution—Voltaire, Rousseau, or the Encyclopedists—" No persons ever cause a revolution; they make themselves, just as storms occur from accumulated vapours, or diseases from corrupted juices and neglect; when the element of discontent manifests itself, the usual course is to meet it by perverse and wrong measures, by which the symptoms are increased and strengthened instead of allayed; then come men who take advantage of the crisis, either from selfishness or the reverse, as they happen to be self-seekers, idealists, or patriots. When the storm bursts those in office lose their heads, and cowardice, the associate of an evil conscience, confuses the understanding. Thereupon follow false measures by which the danger is increased, the flight of those whose duty it is to be at their post, or the wavering of some who, instead of acting with decision, remain weak and helpless.

All this follows in quick succession under the influence of the tempest of God which sweeps over the devoted land; for every revolution is the assize of the Almighty. His kindness is shown in the punishment that He inflicts; for under the terror caused by the angel who directs the storm, all injustice and obsolete usages crumble and fall with a mighty crash; and though many, both good and bad, are crushed and destroyed under the ruins, a new and more perfect edifice arises, and an epoch is marked in the progress of man towards perfection.

As the present notice of Stein and his Reforms is meant to be a popular account for the information of all those who may be interested in the inevitably forthcoming land reforms in England, we think that we cannot do better than complete the Stein-Hardenberg legislation by an addition of that of 1850. We quote from the Cobden Essays above alluded to.

The Legislation of 1850.

The legislation of 1850 was in the highest degree prolific; but we need only concern ourselves with the two great laws of the 2nd March.

1. The Law for the Redemption of Services and Dues, and the Regulation of the Relations between the Lords of the Manor and their Peasants.

2. The Law for the Establishment of Rent Banks.

The former of these laws abrogated the " dominum directum," or overlordship of the lords of the manor, without compensation; so that from the day of its publication, all hereditary holders throughout the Prussian monarchy, irrespectively of the size of their holdings, became proprietors, subject however to the customary services and dues, which, by the further provisions of the law, were commuted into fixed money rents, calculated on the average money value of the services and dues rendered and paid during a certain number of years preceding. By a further provision these rent-charges were made compulsorily redeemable, either by the immediate payment of a capital equivalent to an 18 years' purchase of the rent-charge, or by a payment of $4\frac{1}{2}$ or 5 per cent. for $56\frac{1}{12}$ or $41\frac{1}{12}$ years, on a capital equivalent to 20 years' purchase of the rent-charge.

The law for the establishment of rent banks provided the machinery for this wholesale redemption. By it the State, through the instrumentality of the rent banks, constituted itself the broker between the peasants by whom the rents had to be paid, and the landlords who had to receive them.

The bank established in each district advanced to the latter in rent debentures, paying 4 per cent. interest, a capital sum equal to 20 years' purchase of the rent. The peasant, along with his ordinary rates and taxes, paid into the hands of the district tax collector each month one-twelfth part of a rent calculated at 5 or $4\frac{1}{2}$ per cent. on this capital sum, according as he elected to free his property from encumbrance in $41\frac{1}{12}$ or $56\frac{1}{12}$ years, the respective terms within which, at compound interest the 1 or the $\frac{1}{2}$ per cent., paid in addition to the 4 per cent. interest on the debenture, would extinguish the capital.

The account given of these rent banks in Mr. Hutton's pamphlet, p. 18, is so clear and exhaustive, that it would be lost labour to attempt to improve on it here.

The legislation of 1850 was no more than the efficacious application of the principles contained in the edict of 1811. At first sight two new principles appear to have been introduced—viz., the absence of compensation for the " dominum directum," and the elimination of the principle of payments in land. But if we look at the matter more closely, these differences amount to little. The " dominum directum," as before observed, deprived of its material contents—*i.e.*, of the services and dues, was absolutely valueless to the overlord, whilst, on the other hand, the immediate and simultaneous entrance into full proprietary rights on the part of the many thousands of holders who were affected by the law of the 2nd of March, was calculated to exercise a moral effect of the greatest magnitude.

As regards the non-commutation in land, it will be remembered that the edict of 1811 laid down the rule that the services of holdings less than fifty Prussian acres in size should be commuted in rent-charge only. Now it is probable that most of the holdings over this size had been redeemed prior to 1850, so that practically the law of the 2nd March had only to deal with the smaller kinds of holdings, for which the commutation of services by a rent-charge had been provided by the edict of 1811. It was not by the newness of the principles therefore, but by the incomparably superior machinery for applying the principles, that the legislation of 1850 established its superiority over that of 1811, and obtained such much larger results in comparatively so short a time.

We have now given a general outline of the whole of the Stein-Hardenberg land reforms, as well as the subsequent legislation with regard to the land question in Prussia up to the present time.

Besides these important reforms it is well known that Stein reorganized the whole system of administration in Prussia; he saw clearly that the real intrinsic strength of a nation lies in a moral and independent population, and thus the ground principle of his system was to improve the abject state of the people and raise them from the wretchedness in which they had so long languished, and this he effected by his land reform, whereby a large class of peasant proprietors was created, who, having property and consequently a stake and interest in the State, were far more valuable citizens than feudal slaves who could not call even their souls their own.

It is not our purpose to enter into the merits of his general reforms in the Administration; it is well known that, substantially, they remain law in Prussia at the present day.

In 1814 Stein entered Paris with the Allies, and from that time his power may be said nearly to have ceased, for his views of constitutional liberty were anything but pleasing to the despots of the Vienna Congress, and his weak and ungrateful master the King of Prussia, whom he served so faithfully, at once seems entirely to have forgotten him; the orange had been sucked, and now the rind was to be cast away. Absolutism was far more to the taste of an hereditary Prussian Monarch, and to this he returned as soon as he could; quite forgetting all the bitter lessons of adversity, he preferred his fancied interests to the general good of the people.

Napoleon had fallen, and deservedly—but alas! all hope of progress and liberty which was expected, and which might have accrued, from the

French Revolution, sunk with him to the ground, and poor Europe relapsed once more into the stagnation of absolutism.

Saint Augustine truly said, "*Deus patiens quia æternus*" (God is patient because He is eternal), but wretched man is obliged to be so without the eternity here below to console him; he must learn that the Divine will has decreed that the march of progress should be slow, and he must submit himself to the law. Nature cares not for individuals, but it preserves the species; this seems hard on the individual indeed, but it is inevitable, and many see in it a strong proof of a future, when all inequalities, all inconsistencies, shall be reconciled, and "death swallowed up in victory." Never had man such opportunities as Napoleon, and never did man more abuse and throw them away by his insane and ignoble lust for power. All things doubtless will eventually come right, but that such an opportunity as that granted to Napoleon should have been so lost, and the course of human progress retarded for full sixty years, is a most disheartening reflection for those who have lived during the reaction caused by his selfishness, and who, from their age, may not live to see the coming emancipation of nations from the iron rule of self-seeking despotism.

So long as France waged war against Absolutism—

> "Who of all the Despots banded,
> With that faithful chief competed,
> Who could brood o'er France defeated,
> Till lone tyranny commanded,
> Till goaded by Ambition's wing
> The Hero sunk into the King?
> Then he fell—so perish all
> Who would men by man enthrall."

The German, Heine, says in a work (formerly suppressed but just now published), "It was not merely Frenchmen and the Emperor who succumbed at Waterloo. The French indeed fought for their hearths and homes, but they were at the same time the sacred cohorts who represented the Revolution; the Emperor fought not only for his throne, but also for the flag of the Revolution which he bore—he was the standard-bearer of the democracy, while Wellington on the contrary bore the ensign of the aristocracy."

There is some truth in this, but it is not all correct, for if Napoleon had conquered he would most certainly have gone back to absolutism; the cause of his fall was his having betrayed the cause of the Revolution: we deny that he fought for the people at Waterloo. He fought for his own selfish ends, and well it was for the world that he was conquered. The people of Europe, however, were too ignorant to understand the situation, and thus they fought and conquered under the auspices of those who (not one whit better than Napoleon) were merely desirous of getting power firmly into their own hands. The people were, in fact, very much like those dogs which we see carrying a whip which is frequently to be used over their own backs.

Lord Byron saw this plainly when, on July 7th, 1815, he wrote to Moore:—" Every hope of a Republic is over, and we must go on under the old system." Napoleon was only put down at the cost of sixty years further absolutism for Europe, and which is by no means extinct at the present day on the Continent.

But happily the dark clouds of superstition and ignorance in Europe are being gradually dispersed by the bright sun of science which is now very apparent above the horizon; men begin seriously to *think;* and from thought to action the interval is not very great.

The Land Question in England.

There are certain inalienable natural rights, and among them the greatest is the right to labour and to inherit the land. Latterly the people of England, who have been long languishing in darkness, have seen a great light—a light has arisen upon those who have long been wandering in the valley of the shadow of death. With regard to the land the people of England stand alone in the face of Europe. Richard Cobden, in one of his annual addresses to his constituents at Rochdale, remarked :—" The English peasantry has no parallel on the face of the earth—you have no other peasantry like that of England; you have no other country in which it is *entirely divorced from the land.* There is no other country in the world where you will not find men turning up the furrow in their own freehold. You will not find that in England." This is our starting-point—the people are divorced from the land. If this be true, it follows that they must have been at one time married to the land; and we will now shortly narrate the history of the divorce.

How the People of England became Divorced from the Land.

At the Norman Conquest a fresh survey and partition of the land was made by the Conqueror, who remodelled the land laws, and finally established that feudal system of which even now the traces remain; and it was maintained in full vigour into the sixteenth century, at the commencement of which the great agricultural reforms, commencing at the latter end of the fifteenth century, were in full operation.

The feudal system was by no means so

tyrannical as has been generally supposed—it was very similar to that of Prussia in 1807, when Stein commenced his great work.

England, it may be said, was separated into a vast number of townships; there was a lord of the manor, and a custom of the manor which varied in some respects in different counties, but generally speaking, the rights of the lord as well as of the peasant cultivators, were had *the right of use in the land,* were clearly defined. So long as the peasants performed their feudal services, the chief of which consisted in the gratuitous cultivation of the manor farm, the lord could not deprive them of the use of the soil by the cultivation of which they obtained a livelihood. The villani, or villeins, were sometimes very well-to-do persons, and far happier and more independent than the wretched *real* serfs of the present time with their miserable pittance of from 8s. to 10s. per week.

Each township formed a little community; outside the town was distributed in parcels the arable land in a circle, and beyond this was the common pasture, and beyond this again the constant pasture and woods. No live hedges were to be seen as at the present day, and few ditches; so jealous were the peasants of their rights that it was necessary to put up temporary fences to protect the growing crops, and these fences were invariably demolished on St. Peter's day (13th August, O.S.). The whole village community regularly turned out on that day and demolished them, after which the stubble land remained the property of all alike until the next seedtime, when the dead fences were erected afresh.

But in the fifteenth century certain changes in the conditions of the world manifested themselves; a foreign trade sprung up, particularly in wool, for the production of which the English climate was most favourable, and a great impulse was likewise given to this trade by the discovery of vast quantities of silver in the American mines, which, in the shape of money, afforded a far more convenient medium for exchange than the system hitherto of barter of commodities. Sheep-farming became the rage, and from this time may be dated the commencement of the divorce of the British peasant from the land.

Knowledge is power, but how deplorable it is to see that, not only in England but in all countries, the higher and more intellectual classes have always used that weapon to oppress and enslave the proletariat. A light broke upon the lords of the manor; they discovered that *the system of farming the land in common was a most wasteful method of cultivation, and that the land, when permanently enclosed, would produce full double the quantity for harvest;* and also that sheep-farming under the new circumstances was much more profitable *for themselves* than the continued cultivation of the land in common by the peasantry; and henceforward their endeavours were directed to the expulsion of the people from their manors in order to lay down the land in grass. The lords of the manors would not admit that the peasant had any vested right in the land; on the contrary they said that the land was theirs, and that the peasant only cultivated it so long as they pleased on sufferance; as long as it was to the interest of the landlord the peasant was preserved on the land—when this interest ceased he was regarded as only fit to be exterminated. The truth of this can be proved by numberless writings of the time which are still extant; "to drive poor people from their dwellings they consider no crime, but say the land is theirs, and then cast them out like vermin," says one of these, and Latimer, in a celebrated sermon before Edward VI., said that "the great lords made dowerless slaves of the godly English yeomanry." So great was the exasperation of the people at the continued tyranny of the landlords immediately after the death of Henry VIII. that the Protector Somerset caused a Royal Commission to investigate the grievances of the people. But the weak Government of those days was no match against the power of the provincial nobility and gentry; the matter was brought before Parliament, but the people obtained no redress. Frequent insurrections took place, which succeeded at first, but finally they were all suppressed; for an ignorant populace, however much in the right, never can succeed permanently against intellectual power. All history shows this, and we see it most prominently exemplified in the peasant wars of the sixteenth century in Germany. Right, justice, virtue, goodness and piety, when leagued with ignorance, always succumb to the tyranny and injustice which know how to enlist intellect on their side.

It is the fashion with many historians to call these insurrections of the peasantry rebellion, when the truth is they were merely standing up for their own rights against tyranny; the cause of freedom and right no doubt will conquer finally, but not before numerous individuals have perished in the struggle. This rooting out the poorer class from their holdings has continued down to our own times, and when the high-handed proceedings of the middle ages could no longer be resorted to, legal chicanery stepped in to complete that which mediæval oppression had left unfinished. This was done by means of the iniquitous enclosure acts, a species of legal robbery of which, in May 1845, Lord Lincoln observed in the House of Commons: "This I know, that in nineteen cases out of twenty, committees sitting in this House on private bills neglect the rights of the poor;" in most cases judgment may be said to have gone by default, as it is called, because the poor proprietors could not fee expensive counsel or pay witnesses.

Such is a brief relation of the divorce of the English people from the land and soil which robbed them of their inalienable rights to its cultivation, deprived the nation of that independent class which is so necessary towards maintaining the greatness of an Empire, and is now causing such discontent and demoralization. But there is always a certain Nemesis which follows sooner or later any breach of the natural law. The Greeks had a proverb:—

'Οφε θεῶν ἀλέουσι μύλοι, ἀλέουσι δὲ λεπτά,

which an American poet has utilized in one of his effusions without acknowledgment:

" The mills of God grind slowly, but they grind exceeding small,"

and there is great truth in the saying.

But in judging of the conduct of the English lords of the manor during this great agricultural revolution we must be just and not too severe upon them. It must be recollected that the English movement commenced nearly three centuries ago, while the German reform happened in our days. The difference of enlightenment between the two periods must be taken into consideration, and then perhaps we shall see the reason why justice was done to the peasant in Germany, while in England he was treated with the greatest injustice and cruelty. The difference in the times affords some, though anything but a sufficient, excuse for the English lords of the manor; gross ignorance of the rights of man may mitigate though it cannot excuse their conduct; it was partly a blunder, which, politically speaking, is really often more pernicious than a positive crime.

The selfish error of lords of the manor in driving the population from the land, is shown by all history to be a sin against the natural law for the wellbeing and happiness of a nation, and as a consequence, against political economy. We hear persons talk of true and false political economy, but this is an incorrect mode of expression; there can be no such thing as a false political economy, because then it would not be political economy at all. Political economy is an exact science admitting of no variation any more than the laws of nature, and the only question here is, what is the law of political economy with regard to the land? Let us examine this question more closely, taking the examples of history as well as the light of nature for our guides. A profound German writer on Political Economy says:

"The essential characteristic of a desert is uniformity; a vast expanse of land with no considerable elevations or deep hollows to vary the same dead level, so that no accumulation of atmospheric moisture can be retained. The particles of sand of nearly equal size which form its surface are easily set in motion by every considerable wind of the heavens, so that no vegetation can take firm root; and in this state we see a true type of the economical and political results of an *extreme* equality in the division both of the land and national income of a nation. The opposite extreme is when a middle class of small proprietors has disappeared, and a nation may then be described as consisting of a few rich, and a numerous proletariat. Such a state may be termed a Plutoligarchy which always has a reverse side of pauperism, with all the oppression of an aristocracy *without its advantages;* men are reckoned as of no account, capital alone is held to be of any value. By this state of things the independence of a people is destroyed, as they have neither capital nor land, and are consequently constrained to bring their labour to market to those few who have the command of employment and who can make their own terms. Thus all self-dependence is eliminated from the people, and one of the greatest of moral temptations arises, for the homeless poor will be as prone to hate the law as the rich to hold it in contempt.

"Hence arises the highly contagious power of Communism, its danger to order and freedom.

"There is a terrible example in history of six persons who possessed half the Roman dominions in Africa; Nero caused them all to be murdered." *

A Plutoligarchy—a state to which we are now very fast approaching in England—will always be weak abroad; the great multitude who have nothing to lose will generally care little for the continuance of political independence, if, indeed, they will not rejoice in the

---

* Pliny, "Hist. Nat.," xviii. 7.

fall of their oppressors, hoping to better themselves from the catastrophe. The joy with which the French were welcomed as deliverers in Berlin in 1807, is a proof of this.

Such are the opposite extremes; the parcelling out of the land into exclusively small holdings, and the division of the country among a few large proprietors. Now, what does political economy teach? It teaches that harmony in a State can only be lastingly secured when the land is fairly divided into large, medium, and especially into small peasant holdings. History also teaches that the excrescence of a Plutocracy—the sure sign of declining life in a nation—has always been a stumbling block to the legislator from the most ancient times.

If we look to the history of the Hebrew kings we find the prophets denouncing Plutocracy, thus: Amos vi. 1—"*Woe to them that are at ease in Zion, and trust in the mountain of Samaria, which are named chief of the nations, to whom the house of Israel came.*" And Micah

ii. 2—"*And they covet fields, and take them by violence; and houses, and take them away; so they oppress a man and his house, even a man and his heritage.*" And again, Isaiah v. 8—"*Woe unto them that join house to house, that lay field to field, till there be no place, that they may be placed alone in the midst of the earth.*"

And in later times if we refer back to ancient Greece we see that "*Men of fortune extended their estates without bounds, not scrupling to exclude the rightful heirs, and the whole property coming into the hands of the few, the rest were poor and miserable.* These finding no time or opportunity to learn and exercise the liberal arts, were obliged to drudge in mean and mechanic employments for their daily bread, and consequently looked with envy and hatred on the rich. There remained not above seven hundred of the old Spartan families, of which, perhaps, one hundred had estates in land. The rest of the city was filled with an insignificant rabble without property or honour, who had neither heart nor spirit to defend their country against wars abroad, and who were always watching an opportunity for change at home."*

If any further historical testimony were necessary to prove the truth of the position, we have only to take France and Prussia—France before the great revolution, and Prussia before her overthrow in 1807. If the landed proprietors in England are not convinced by these precedents, then indeed they would not be convinced even though one arose from the dead. The greater part of the landlords, however, are far from owning that they are convinced of that which appears to them to be against their own interest; on the contrary, some of the highest intellects among them maintain that the present state of land tenure in England is quite right and proper, and especially a very able writer in the *Quarterly Review* has openly spoken against a reform in the land laws. We shall here quote

---

* Plutarch—*Agis*.

his words, and refer our readers to a late article in the organ of the Tories, the *Quarterly Review,* entitled " The Proletariat on the Wrong Scent," by which it is plainly to be seen that the land monopolists have seriously taken the alarm at the prospects of a movement which they conceive will interfere with what they consider their just rights and privileges.

Speaking of the great Reforms of the Baron Stein which we have sketched, Mr. Greg says :—

" We will admit that, since the promulgation of the new system in Prussia by which feudalism was broken up and large estates began to be superseded by smaller ones, the improvement in agriculture and in the condition of the peasant class has been *marked, vast,* and *undeniable.*

" We will concede, moreover, that much of this amelioration is the effect, and the natural and necessary effect, of the change from Proletarism to proprietorship, and that *ceteris paribus* land will always yield more to the hand of the owner than to hired labour.

"But all this is but the first effect of the transition, the question for a philosophic statesman regards a future day and a secondary consequence.

"When the old system shall have been altogether superseded by the new; when the whole of the land shall be in the possession of peasant proprietors; when industry, science, and the due subdivision of the land shall have brought it all into that state of minute and perfect cultivation which we observe in many parts of Lombardy, of Flanders, and of Switzerland, and which two generations of peasant proprietorship suffices to effect—What then? No new estates can be created, for you have reached the limit at which subdivision is compatible with good agriculture or with comfortable subsistence; no more individuals can be supported by the soil, for its utmost yield has been extracted from it; manufacturing establishments have been superseded by articles produced at home; foreign commerce has languished and died under the gradual extinction of exchangeable articles and available surplus for luxurious expenditure, and the Civil and Military services have been reduced to a minimum because only a small revenue can be raised by direct taxation from a nation which consists of one vast class of yeomanry."—*Greg's Essays*, 143.

"One vast class of yeomanry!" This is a mere assumption and not reasoning. Have we not seen Prussia, which has partitioned fully one half the land among the people, great and prosperous—a nation which, from a vicious system of government, founded on a false idea of political economy, had sunk into a state of the greatest degradation and misery—a nation which old Fritz himself, after he had drilled it into a perfect state of automatonism, admitted was nothing more than a mere aggregation of slaves,—and one able man arose, and by the simple expedient of planting the people on the soil from which they had been divorced,—by simply turning serfs into landed proprietors,—succeeded in raising this country from her ashes; and his success is described by Mr. Greg as "marked, vast, and undeniable;" and though seventy years have flown since this success, and the nation has risen to the pinnacle of earthly power and greatness, we are told that this is only the first effect of the transition! and that the question for a philosophic statesman regards a future day, and a secondary consequence!

Where, we ask, is the one vast class of Yeomanry in Prussia which should be there according to Mr. Greg's theory?

In a late essay published by the Cobden Club, by Mr. Grant Duff, on the teaching of Richard Cobden, he says: "Free trade applied to land —nothing more nor nothing less"—this was all Cobden proposed! Now these were the last words of Richard Cobden with regard to the and; he had before said that "divorce from the soil was a national calamity and a disgrace." In his last speech he said:

"The English peasantry has no parallel on the face of the earth; you have no other country in which it is entirely divorced from the land. There is no other country in the world where you will not find men turning up the furrow on their own freehold!" Is it not clear from this that Cobden thought that in England also the "peasant should have his own freehold;" and I would ask Mr. Grant Duff how this can possibly be brought about by simple free trade in land?*

Lord A. and manufacturer B. buy up a whole county; they take all the land, and subject it to the law of entail; and where I ask is the peasant to get his freehold?† If, instead of the artificial means by which Stein planted the Prussian peasant on the soil, he had simply proclaimed free trade in the land, where would Prussia have been now? If Cobden were alive

---

* Since this was written, Mr. Cobden's remarkable letter has been published by Mr. J. Bright. *Vide* Appendix (D).

† *Vide* Appendix (F).

he would have seen how utterly futile such an expedient would have been towards carrying out his views. Cobden advocated free trade in land as well as in everything else, and so do we; but in Cobden's time the land question was only just, as seamen say, heaving in sight; people were only becoming awake to the importance of the question, which Cobden had examined in all its bearings. Certainly he had too much sound sense to complain that peasant proprietors were wanted, which he undeniably did, and then at the same time deprecate the means of forming them; his letter settles this point. (Ap. D.)

A few persons take the whole of the land, as in Scotland,* and then say, Oh! free trade in land,—when the whole of it has been monopolized. No, without some artificial means, without some Government help, nothing can be effectually done to increase the small holders.

But then the question comes: What is to be

---

* *Vide* Appendix (G).

done, and who is to do it? Where are we to find our Stein? We have one well capable of following in his steps, and that is John Bright. We see that he has withstood the temptations of rank and power, before which so many men, even the most gifted, succumb. He knows, to use the words of Stein, " dass nur Der sich rühmen darf, einen guten Kampf gekämpft zu haben, den beharret bis aus ende."*

Stein believed that the souls of the departed were permitted to look down and still take an interest in the affairs of this world; may we not fancy the spirit of the good Cobden joyfully looking down on the present aspect of the land-question agitation in England?

Many think that it is too late, that the time has gone by never to be recalled; that we should have made the reform *à la Stein* in the reign of Henry VIII.; and that to again create a

---

* He alone can boast of having fought the good fight who remains till the end of the battle.

yeoman class is quite a hopeless task. If this be true, then all we can say is, that the country is very far down on the inclined plane which leads to destruction. But we have better hopes. We think better of the stamina of the English people. On their efforts all depends, for from the landlords they have nothing to hope. Neither can they rely on a House of Commons constituted like the present one. An assembly consisting of landowners and the rich will never restore the land which has been wrested from the poorer cultivators. No palliative remedies will have any permanent effect here; the cottage and allotment system would be useless. The only remedy is an *extension of the suffrage to the agricultural labourer;* then we may hope to have men returned to Parliament pledged to a thorough land reform *à la Stein,* and not till then.

There would be no injustice whatever in this. In Prussia there are large, medium, and small proprietors, and there is *not* that overwhelming preponderance of yeomanry which no doubt would be pernicious, exactly as we see it is at this moment in France.

The first steps for a comprehensive land reform in England would be the abolition of the laws of primogeniture and entails, the removal of all impediments to the transfer of land, and the utilization by the legislature of all wastes to form small properties. This, together with the acquirement by purchase of such other land as might be thought requisite, and the division of it into small holdings, would again plant the people on the land from which they have been so unjustly driven; and then again we may see our beautiful country dotted with the peaceful homes of small peasant proprietors, and England once more " merry" (a sad misnomer now); and if we have not so many large landed proprietors, at any rate we shall have established a happy and moral class of contented yeomanry, which will form a most important addition to the material and intrinsic strength of the nation.

Here we might have brought this short sketch to an end, but as there is no life of Stein in the English language, we trust our readers will excuse us if we complete our sketch by following up the career of that remarkable man to its close.

On the 31st March, 1814, the allies entered Paris, and the great war of deliverance from the yoke of Napoleon was at an end. On the 9th April Stein arrived in Paris. At length the day had arrived;—the gloomy clouds which had so long obscured the destiny of Prussia had all melted away; success beyond the hopes of his wildest imagination had come to cheer his heart after years of the most bitter humiliation; his most heartfelt gratitude was due to Providence which had vouchsafed such blessings to his beloved Fatherland, and to Alexander, its chosen instrument for carrying out its wise plans.

Such were Stein's feelings, mixed up with a most profound contempt for Napoleon and the French nation. We see it proved in his letters which were written at this period, and from which the following is extracted:—

"Thank heaven for this happy event—the man (Napoleon) lies prostrate, for which we owe eternal gratitude to the Emperor Alexander. The tyrant has closed his career as a coward. As long as he could shed the blood of others with impunity he stinted not his hand, but when the day of trial came courage was wanted to face death. To save his wretched life he spares neither tears nor supplications; to prolong his miserable existence he descends to the meanest arts;—what a contemptible monster! All hearts, on the contrary, are captivated by the demeanour of the Emperor Alexander. His whole proceedings may be described as a union of wisdom, nobility, courage, and loftiness of soul. This shameless, impure, and immoral French race are already abusing his generosity, they can only be ruled with an iron sceptre. How disgusting it is to hear them, after having covered themselves with crime, talking of their honesty, goodness, and magnanimity, just as if Europe had not been filled with blood and mourning by their acts, and as if they had not murdered three kings within two centuries, and on all occasions evinced the most repulsive greed. Napoleon went out hunting on the 9th; he only thinks of his ordinary pleasures. The same meanness of spirit which he showed in his flight from Russia, when he left his army a prey to cold and hunger, makes his present position endurable. The Archduchess (Marie Louise) goes back to her father, Jerome to Stuttgart, Joseph to Switzerland, so the whole pack of ragamuffins is annihilated."

This extract clearly shows how little Stein was acquainted with human nature; we shall soon see how bitterly he was disappointed when, his illusions dissipated, he found out the real character of the Tartuffe Emperor Alexander, as he has been justly called, at the Vienna Congress, where Germany was completely thrown over, and went empty away. Stein's idea was the formation of a united Germany, but he soon found that the Emperor Alexander was very far from supporting his views, he being solely intent on securing as much of the spoil as he could lay his hands upon. The Congress of Vienna may be compared to a swarm of hungry vultures fighting over a carcase, each trying to gorge its utmost.

Stein was indefatigable in his endeavours to establish his views for a united Germany before the Congress, but the opposing interests and selfishness of Austria, Bavaria, and the whole host of petty German princes, foiled all his plans, till, as a last resource, he proposed the re-establishment of a German empire as his sheet-anchor, his last hope. All was, however, vain, although the Emperor of Russia, and Wessenberg, one of the Austrian plenipotentiaries, supported him. Metternich, the Emperor of Austria, as well as Bavaria and Würtemberg, and (*mirabile dictu*), the representatives of Prussia, decidedly opposed his proposition. The memorial of Stein to the

Emperor Alexander for the establishment of an Empire was opposed by a counter memorial by Humboldt, who represented that the dignity of an Emperor without corresponding power would be merely an object of jealousy and discord,— with corresponding power, would tend to circumscribe that of the large States, and especially Prussia, who never would submit to such a subjection. Hardenberg (!) also inclined to this latter view. Stein had recourse to Wellington, and tried to gain him over to his views for a German Empire, but without success, and the Emperor Alexander, seeing such a preponderance of opinion against him, gave way, and decided that a German Empire was impracticable. Thus, finding all his efforts fruitless, Stein indignantly withdrew from any further interference with the Vienna Congress.

The return of Napoleon from Elba quickly brought the work of the Congress to a close. The news reached Vienna on 7th March, and the Congress closed its sittings on the 9th June.

Stein had left Vienna on the 28th May, profoundly disappointed at the failure of all his plans, and with bitter feelings against Hardenberg and Humboldt for the part which they had taken against him. The course of events during the hundred days is well known. Stein declared decidedly for the restoration of the Bourbons. He had retired to Nassau for the benefit of the baths, as his health had become affected: but he proceeded to Paris on the 14th August, and at once used all his energies to obtain better terms for his country under the changed conditions of parties, but all interests were against him. England and Russia considered that Prussia's weakness was their gain, his memorials were neglected and his projects defeated, all hope of forming an United Germany lost, and the well-merited independence of his Fatherland shipwrecked by the interests of the Great Powers, joined to the lust for rule and selfish spirit of the petty German princes.

Deeply disgusted, and with an especially bitter

feeling against the Emperor Alexander, whose selfishness and duplicity he now fully saw through, Stein retired from the contest; and here we may say he disappears from the page of political history. He lived fifteen years from this period, but exercised no influence on the further progress of events. The Emperor Alexander offered him a position in the Russian service, which was declined. Feeling he could work no longer for his country, the rest of his life was passed in retirement; but, notwithstanding the repeated failure of his plans for the unity of Germany, his faith in the final triumph of good over the principle of evil, and a Divine superintendence of this world, was never shaken. This is proved by his own words in 1816, when in conversation with a friend, he said, "Yes, my dear friend, we have gained much, but many things should have been very different from what they are. God rules the world and will not desert the Germans if they remain true to themselves. They will in future be able to hold their own well against the

French." After a short silence he added: " I long to be at rest; this world is so constituted that we cannot for the most part progress on the straight road, and crooked paths are forbidden. Yes, the truth is that circumstances and conditions urge and drive mankind; they act and purpose; they do it, but God decides."

Here we see the expression of Stein's religious views, to which we shall have to allude in the sequel. *They* do it, but *God* decides. This is exactly the "*Les hommes agissent, mais Dieu les mène*" of Bossuet. Men act, but God leads them; which often quoted dictum, if it be put to the test of simple common sense, will be found to be simple nonsense. How can men possibly act if God leads them? If God leads men it is He that acts; man has no choice in the matter. But Stein never got over what his mother told him, and never used his reason in these matters.* If he had possessed a little more living experience he

---

* Appendix (H).

would have known that, in human affairs, justice is really one of the very last of all considerations. He hoped that the affairs of Germany would at any rate meet with some kind of justice, some little equity; but as a German historian well remarks: " Thörichte Hoffnung, gegründet auf den unter dem Volke der Geduld hartnäckig heimischen ' ideologischen ' Glauben ; es sei nur eine misanthropische Grille, zu glauben, dass nicht die arme heimatlose Gerechtigkeit, sondern vielmehr das höllische Kleeblatt Selbstsucht, Schufterei und Gewaltsamkeit die Weltregiere."*

In the affairs of nations as well as in those of individuals, to be weak is to be in the wrong. No representations, no memorials, and no prayers are ever efficacious unless supported by material force—*preces armatæ* are the only ones that ever gain a response. Tyranny and cowardice

---

* Most insensate of all hopes! founded on the fantastic homebred faith that the world is governed by poor homeless justice, and that it is merely a misanthropic caprice to imagine that it is ruled by the hellish triad of egotism, baseness, and brute force!

are twin brothers, and it is in vain to supplicate the former unless you have the power to threaten the latter. There is a very profound truth as well as intimate knowledge of human nature in the scene from Molière's play of *Les Précieuses Ridicules,* where Stein represents the 1st Porter, and the Emperor Alexander, Mascarille. Alas! Stein had no strong comrade for a 2nd Porter.

> *Emperor* (Mascarille).—There, take yourself off with your chair.
> *Stein* (Porter).—Please, your honour, to pay me my fare.
> *Emperor* (Mascarille).—What, you rascal! ask for payment from a man of my quality? [*Gives him a box on the ear.*]
> *Stein* (Porter).—Ah! that's the way we poor fellows get paid. Will your quality give me my dinner, I wonder?
> *Emperor* (Mascarille).—I'll teach such low scoundrels as you to know your place!

And Stein did at last know his place; too late he saw that he had no force to back his just demand. He fondly believed in the "direct path" and in "worldly justice." How different would it have been if his brother Porter, the King of Prussia, had been in a position to have played the part of the 2nd Porter in Molière's scene thus :—

> 2nd *Porter* (King of Prussia) (taking one of the poles of the chair, and confronting Alexander).— I say, Mr. Emperor, pay us our fare in less than no time.
> *Emperor* (Mascarille).—Eh ? what ?
> 2nd *Porter.*—I say, stump up the fare—quick!
> *Emperor* (Mascarille).—Ah! I see you can be reasonable. There is some sense in the way you put it.
> 2nd *Porter* (King of Prussia).—Come, we can't wait— the fare!
> *Emperor* (Mascarille).—Oh, certainly! You speak like a man, but your companion there is an ass who does not know how to speak! There, there is your fare. Are you satisfied now?
> 2nd *Porter.*—No, you struck my comrade. [*Threatens him with his pole.*]
> *Emperor* (Mascarille).—Stop, there's for the box on the car! A person can get anything from me if he only goes the right way to work about it.

If Stein had possessed sufficient penetration to have seen through this constant peculiarity of human nature, he would not have had to complain in his bitterness that he had been completely deceived in his trust in German sympathies, English disinterestedness, and the magnanimity of the Emperor Alexander. This last consideration gave him the greatest pain; he had looked on Alexander as a miracle of noble self-denial and disinterestedness, as a chosen and worthy instrument of the Almighty for the emancipation of Europe and the establishment of German Unity, and now he discovered that he was nothing more than a mere Russian autocrat, who had no sympathy with the other European Powers, and who cared for nothing but his own interests.

Stein retired to an estate which had been conferred on him in Prussian Westphalia, near Dortmund, and spent his time in superintending his property, and in local affairs. In 1819 he was most painfully stricken by the loss of his wife, who died on the 15th Sept., leaving him with two daughters, who both married, in 1825, and 1827, thus leaving him quite solitary. In 1828 he was attacked by severe illness, from which he never completely recovered; he suffered much at times from asthma, and also complained of great loss of memory, which, however, was not apparent to his friends; he became irritable about small matters with regard to his property, and enjoyed nothing but the contemplation of the beauties of nature, contrasting them with the wild excesses of mankind, and generally wound up such contemplations with the words, "I wish I were well out of it—the earth seems to me like a large graveyard—first one and then another friend disappears—I stand alone, and the rising generation no longer understands me— we are coming on troublous times—God is preparing a fearful judgment on the world; if I were young I would take my part in the struggle, but old and decrepit as I am, I am doomed to be a mere looker on."

In 1831 he felt that he had not long to live; he suffered from gout, and had several apoplectic attacks. On 21st June he was overtaken by a heavy storm of rain, and came home completely wet through; a cold accompanied by fever followed, and he told his medical attendant that he thought his death was at hand. He now ordered, if Providence should decree his death, that: 1st. His body should be embalmed to keep it from corruption. 2nd. That the coffin should be drawn by his own horses to the family vault. 3rd. That a metal plate should be placed on the lid of the coffin engraved with his name and his age. On the 23rd June he appeared a little better, but still maintained his conviction that he would go off suddenly of pectoral apoplexy. "I fear not death," said he, "I know what I am worth in the eyes of God, I am a poor sinner and can only obtain salvation through the merits of my Redeemer." Towards evening he became very restless and impatient. He begged to hear a discourse on death instead of the usual evening prayers. On being reminded of Christian patience, he sighed. "Ah, Christian patience," he repeated, and for the rest of the day he remained calm, patient, and amiable as ever.

On Sunday 26th, one of Emmerich's sermons was read to him, the text was: " Come all ye who are heavily laden." Stein expressed his thanks for the choice of the text, and said that Emmerich's sermons always gave him the greatest comfort and peace of mind. On the 28th his weakness sensibly increased; at two o'clock sudden and violent fever with determination of blood to the head and heart set in, and he expressed a wish that the Sacrament should be administered to him.

At ten he took leave of all his dependents. As his steward, Poock, approached the bed, he caused himself to be raised up, and clasping both his hands, said: "Farewell, my dear Poock, I feel that my end is at hand; you have always been a faithful servant to me, and have merited my gratitude; it is my wish that you should serve my children with the same honesty and fidelity with which you have served me." Here Poock interrupted him. " I hope and wish with all my heart that your Excellency will be restored to health; but if it should please God to rule otherwise, and call you to his heavenly kingdom, I promise you that I will serve your heirs and successors with the same fidelity and devotion that I have your Excellency."

Stein then continued: "I have left my property to my daughters, my wishes are that everything should go on as far as possible as formerly, and that the distribution of alms and subscriptions should continue to be apportioned as heretofore. Tell my children this, and aid them in carrying it out. Do you hear me? Forget it not, it is my will.

"Further, I must tell you that it is my firm belief that there is an eternal union between the living and the dead, and it will afford me pleasure when I look down on you from above, to see you show to my children the same fidelity and attachment that you have done to me."

Here the steward again interrupted him, "I also believe in that eternal union, and I feel convinced beforehand, that my conduct towards the children of your Excellency will give you joy in another world." As the steward retired, Stein stretched out his hand to him and said, "We shall meet again in another world; bear my remembrances to your wife and family. Then all the other servants came in their turn. His serene spirit rose superior to the weakness of his body; never had he been known to speak so clearly and with such eloquence; he had something to say to each individual, remembering even their smallest merits, and bidding them to be true and faithful to his children, recommending them all to lead a religious and moral life, and advising them to be true and industrious in their calling. To one of the young gamekeepers he said: "If a war breaks out, mind you fight like a brave Prussian for your king and country." He then forgave them all, requested their forgiveness, and dismissed them with the hope of a future joyful meeting beyond the grave.

It was now three o'clock and the arrival of the clergyman was announced. Stein caused himself to be raised up in his bed, and stretching out his hand said: "Herr Pastor, I appear before you as a poor sinner who desires to acknowledge his sins and become reconciled to his Redeemer by means of the Holy Sacrament." After he had received it and had rested a moment, he begged to be again lifted up, and extending his hand towards the pastor, he exhorted him to increase in the true faith; that the Church being in danger from France, it was necessary for her servants to be on their guard. God had hitherto protected her and would continue to do so." After which, amid the bitter tears of all those standing round his bed, in a faint voice and nearly exhausted, he turned to the physician and asked him if there was any hope, and on receiving a tranquillizing assurance, he was laid down and fell into a soft slumber. About six o'clock in the evening he turned on his left side, a bloodvessel had burst on his lungs, and with one last deep inspiration the spirit of this good man passed away, as he firmly believed, to another and a higher state of existence.

In judging of the character of Stein we must not be carried away by our admiration for his perfectly good and child-like innocence of life; he lived in times of great trouble, and as he never travelled or saw the world as it is outside the narrow sphere in which he lived, he never got over the views in which he had been sedulously educated. History certainly will not give the verdict that he was a great man —he acted according to his lights, he thought that his views were just, and he endeavoured with all the might of his strong will to further them, and when he found that his success was only partial, at the latter end of his life he fell into a gloomy species of fatalism which anything but squared with his orthodox religious persuasions. We see this from a letter to Hövel in 1819. "I must admit to you that the result of my experience in life, especially in the political world, leads to the conclusion of the utter nullity of all human knowledge and actions;" and again in another letter to Gagern, 1821: "I have no confidence in any of the immediate actors in the events of the time, but an unconditional confidence in Providence." A German historian remarks that there was an utter want of the abstract philosophic element as well as of a creative poetical capability in Stein's composition, which was influenced by his early religious education and by custom. Like all unreasoning sectarians he was most bitter against all innovators. In 1818 he wrote to Eichhorn: "When will that wretched rationalism cease in our Protestant Church? Why will people attempt to explain the inexplicable, to unveil the mysterious with their imperfect knowledge and limited powers? A Synodal administration would soon compel our enlightened Protestant divines to retrace their steps and keep within the bounds of simple Christian doctrine. It is not an exegetic twaddle of natural philosophy or a Christo-atheistic cant, but the simple doctrine of Christianity founded on faith, hope, and love which the Germans want and require as a guide through life, and as a refuge and sheet anchor in the hour of death."

Stein was a royalist and an aristocrat, and it is more than doubtful whether he would have worked to emancipate the peasants had he lived in other times. In fact, we have the most positive proof of this when Stein gradually went over to, and took part with, the reactionists in 1819. The following extract from a letter to Niebuhr in 1821 fully bears out this view:—

"I hold, under the present state of the public mind, that the freedom of the press is pernicious; it gives free play for editors avid of gain, to lay all the most weighty affairs of Church and State before the *swinish multitude;* matters which can only be decided by competent and talented individuals should not be mooted at tea-tables, wine-shops, and beer-houses. Freedom of discussion can take place in Parliament, and in earnest well-considered publications; but the licentious tribe of pamphleteers and newspaper writers should be restrained at least till the present wild generation has passed away, and the new institutions have taken firm root.

"The freedom of the citizen must rest on a Church and State administration developed from the history of the people, and not on the rotten foundation of newspapers and pamphlets."

Further, on the appearance of the law for the emancipation of the peasantry in Westphalia, 25th September, 1820, which was precisely what he had himself advocated in Prussia, we see with pain Stein, the admired creator of a free peasant class, one of the most bitter opponents of the carrying out of his own idea; and there can be no mistake about this, for we have his own words:—" To convert feudal service into a money rent which is to cease after a stated time, is a gross attack on the rights of property;" and again, "I reckon this law for the partition of the peasant farms, and freeing them from their connexion with the proprietors, as one of the most pernicious innovations" (to Niebuhr, 1822).

We could multiply these proofs *ad infinitum*

from the voluminous correspondence of Stein which is at our disposal, but we have proved quite enough to show that his reforms were the children of circumstances; and that it is beyond the shadow of a doubt that they never would have been made had not Stein seen that without them there was no hope for a united Germany. He did not live to see the accomplishment of his dearest wishes; but if his creed be true, his spirit is now looking down from the realms above and rejoicing over the triumph of his legislation, which, without doubt, has so largely contributed to the glory and triumphs of his beloved fatherland.

APPENDIX.

A.

When the reaction took place in Prussia, 1815-30, we find with sorrow that all Stein's liberal ideas vanished, and he appears before us as a true aristocrat of the most absolute character. Now that he wanted the services of the people no longer, he called them the " swinish multitude," who were fit for nothing but to hew wood and draw water as vassals of a great lord. But we will let him speak for himself— 20 Decr. 1821, in a letter to Niebuhr,—" I hold that, under the present circumstances of public opinion, the freedom of the press with regard to journals and periodicals is pernicious. A full play is thereby given for disseminating the shallow views of authors greedy of gain, and for mooting questions of the most serious importance to the Church and State, and placing them in a distorted sense before the tribunal of a *swinish multitude.*" These last words appear in English in a parenthesis, thus :—" vor den Richterstuhle des grossen, eitlen, *seichten Haufens* (swinish multitude)."—Stern, 529.

B.

Vide—" The Agricultural Community of the Middle Ages and Inclosures of the Sixteenth Century in England." Translated from the German of E. NASSE, by Col. H. A. Ouvry. 2nd Edition. Williams and Norgate.

C.

The following extract will show the prevailing opinion among the Conservative portion of the German public. It is from the pen of Strauss, and is translated from his recent publication, "The Old and the New Faith :"

" According to the prevailing opinion at the

present time in Germany with regard to the different forms of an administrative Government, the Republic *per se* takes the first place; but under the circumstances and conditions of the great European States, the time has not arrived for the establishment of such a mode of Government, neither can the period be accurately determined as to when it will be advisable to do so; therefore as tolerable a monarchy as possible is preferable.

These views show a considerable advance in comparison with those held some twenty years ago, when a very considerable party in Germany considered a monarchy as untenable, and that the time had arrived to steer directly towards a Republic.

The question however as to which form of Government *per se* is the best, is always looked upon in a false light. It is exactly as if we put the question, what is the best kind of clothing? which cannot be determined without first ascertaining the conditions of climate, season, age, sex, and state of health, &c. There is no such thing as an absolutely best form of Government, because such form is essentially relative ; in the United States, with unlimited space at command, with no dangers to fear from neighbours, and which at the worst is only threatened by party strife from within, a Republic may be a most excellent form of administration. In mountainous Switzerland, the neutrality of which moreover is secured by the self-interest of the neighbouring States, a Republic may also suit admirably ; but for Germany, wedged in between a rapacious Russia, and an unsettled France which is now brooding over revenge, it would be destructive.

Now if we wish to ascertain how opinion goes as to which form of Government is best calculated to sustain the dignity, the nature and destination of man most consistently, in this sense we may say decidedly that it would *not* be that of a Republic.

History as well as experience teaches us that,

at least up to the present time, in Republican States, the destination of man, *i.e.*, the harmonious development of his talents and capabilities, does not appear to be better promoted or advanced than under monarchies. The ancient Republics, all will allow, must here be put out of the question, as they were conditioned by a slave class, and thus may rather be designated exclusive aristocracies. In more recent times Republics are only to be met with in smaller commonwealths, chiefly in towns and urban jurisdictions, and if without absolute slaves, are for the most part administered under the most exclusive aristocratic forms. In modern times we find Republics partly transitory, as in France, where they form the resting places in violent political crises; and partly permanent—on a large scale in North America, on a small one in Switzerland.

No doubt these two Republics (the only ones which are firmly planted) have certain advantages which are common to each. In the first place, the Republican form of Government has obtained the favour of the multitude on account of the lightness of the burdens which are thrown on the citizen, and the more favourable state of its financial conditions, and also his not merely passive, but really active co-operation in the Government. To this may be especially added the freer scope given to individuals for activity and for following out their own inclinations. Yet this has its drawback inasmuch as it opens wide the door for letting in revolutionary political agitation, keeps the country in a perpetual state of fermentation, and impels it on to the inclined plane which unavoidably leads to a continually coarser democracy,—in all cases the very worst form of Government imaginable.

But while we do not despair of being able to limit monarchies by introducing the participation of the citizens in the Government, and allowing them every freedom so long as the constitution is not endangered, in the two above-mentioned Republics we miss that progress of the higher mental interests which we find in monarchical Germany and relatively also in England. Schools and colleges,—and these also well-established and conducted—are to be found both in America and Switzerland; but the higher results are wanting. The Cantons which give the tone in Switzerland are German; in the United States of America, after the English, we see that the German element is the prevailing one; and notwithstanding this, science and art in Switzerland, as well as in North America, have failed to develop those independent blossoms which in Germany and England have been the precursors of a plentiful harvest of good fruits. Switzerland has no indigenous classical literature whatever, and is obliged to come begging to Germany, while all the high places in her colleges are filled either by Germans or those who have received a German education. The literature of North America is in exactly the same relation to that of England, and in so far as this is not the case, we see that science and education take the form of the exact and practical, and tend entirely towards utilitarianism. In short, to us Germans there appears to be something vulgar, something coarse, realistic and prosaically insipid in the mental organization of these two Republics: thrown among them, we feel the want of the rarefied spiritual vital air which we breathed at home; and in America especially we find the atmosphere vitiated by a taint among the classes who take the lead, which is only to be met with in the most neglected parts of Europe. Thus, as we believe that these defects, together with an absence of the feeling of nationality, prevail essentially in the Republican form of Government, we are very far from giving it the preference over that of the monarchical.

It is very certain that the organization of a Republic, even when on a large scale, is more simple and comprehensible than that of a well organized monarchy. The constitution of the Swiss Confederation, not to mention the separate cantons, holds the same relation to that of the English as a water-wheel does to a steam-engine, or as a waltz or a simple air to a fugue or a symphony. There is something enigmatical in a monarchy, we may say something apparently absurd; but in this very fact of mystery lies its advantage. Every mystery appears absurd, and yet nothing is profound, either in a State, in life or in art, without mystery.

That the mere accident of birth should exalt one man over all others, and give him power to rule over the destiny of millions, in spite of the possibility of his possessing a limited capacity of mind or a vicious disposition—that such an accident alone should place him and his family high above so many of his subjects who may be far superior to him, both in intelligence and goodness, appears on the face of the proceeding to be incompatible with the original equality of all mankind, and revolting to common sense; and for this reason such arguments have always been the staple platitudes on democratic platforms. A little more patience and self-denial with a deeper penetration will, however, enable us to see how this setting up an individual and his family on an eminence where he cannot be affected by party struggles or interests, where all doubt is removed as to his authority, and all change except the natural one of death is provided for—and even when this last event occurs, a successor being ready to take his place without election and without struggle,—how materially the strength and happiness of a nation may be permanently secured by the monarchical form of government, and how far superior it is to that of a Republic.

Another thing which favours the monarchical form of government is, that the State is free from the corruptions and disturbances which occur in Republics on account of the constant change in the higher administrative offices which takes place periodically every few years.

But above all, in North America at a presidential election, the unavoidable bribery and corruption, the necessity of rewarding the lower agents employed by giving them government places, and then afterwards being obliged to wink at their unfitness for office, with all the corruption thence accruing among the ruling classes, has somewhat cooled the zeal of the German public in their hopes of finding a political and moral ideal on the far side of the Atlantic Ocean.

To find this on the other side of the Channel would be alike futile, but still we have more and much better things to learn from the English than from the Americans, and, above all, from a due appreciation of the benefits of an hereditary monarchical dynasty for a nation. We might be somewhat alarmed for the political soundness of England on account of the Republican agitation which has lately manifested itself—for that a Republic would certainly be "finis Britanniæ" no sane man would doubt—but behold! the Prince of Wales falls sick, his life is despaired of, and although the nation was far from being satisfied with regard to the conduct and mode of life of the successor to the throne, yet the general sympathy rose to such a degree that even the Republican agitators felt constrained to convey an address containing an expression of condolence to the Queen.

What a sound political instinct do we see here in the English people!—how must the French envy them,—the French, who have rooted out their dynasty with such irreverent haste, and who now, oscillating between despotism and anarchy, can neither live nor yet die."

D.

The following advice to Land Reformers is from the pen of Mr. Mill. It speaks for itself.

Advice to Land Reformers.

Now, when the question of the constitution and limits of property in land has fairly come to the front, and a majority of Liberal politicians finds it needful to include in their programme some improvement in the existing arrangements on that subject, it is time to consider which, among the minor modifications that alone find favour with the more timid or more cautious innovators, deserve to be supported by those who desire greater changes, and which are those that should be opposed, either as giving a renewed sanction to wrong principles, or as raising up new private interests hostile to a thorough reform. There are at present two proposals affecting property in land which engage a considerable and increasing amount of public attention : one, the abrogation of the right of primogeniture, and the abolition or great restriction of the power of making settlements of land; the other, that corporations and endowed institutions should be required to sell their lands, and invest the proceeds in the funds or other public securities. The difference between these two projects affords an illustration of the principles which, we think, should guide the judgment of land tenure reformers in matters of this nature. The former of the two is, in our opinion, entitled to their full support; the latter should be strenuously resisted by them.

Before proceeding farther, it is right to explain whom we mean by land tenure reformers. On so new a question there are naturally many shades of opinion. There are some with whose plans we agree, others from whom we differ; we address ourselves equally to both. There are those who aim at what is called the nationalization of the land; the substitution of collective for individual property in the soil, with reasonable compensation to the landowners. Their doctrine is far from being so irrational as is pretended; they have much to say for themselves. Nor is theirs a wholly untried theory. It has the feudal traditions, and the general practice of the East, on its side. Nevertheless, for reasons which we shall have many opportunities of stating, we are decidedly of opinion that, whatever may possibly be the case in a distant future, this scheme is altogether unsuited to the present time. But, short of this, there are modifications of the rights of landed property of a more or less fundamental character, which have already numerous supporters, and are likely, as we believe, before long to become widely popular. There is the principle asserted by the Land Tenure Reform Association, that, inasmuch as land in a prosperous country brings in a constantly increasing income to its owner, apart from any exertion or expenditure on his part, it may and ought to be subjected to special taxation in virtue of that increase. Again, it is maintained that, inasmuch as the acknowledged end for which land is allowed to be appropriated, is that it may be made more productive, the right of property ought not to extend to that which remains unproductive: and that if large tracts of land are kept in a wild state by their owners, either for purposes of amusement, or because they cannot be let at a rent (though they might amply remunerate a labourer cultivating for himself) the State should resume them, paying only their present value. Again, there might be a limit set to the extent of territory which could be held by a single proprietor. Many other changes might be proposed, more or less extensive, more or less expedient, but all compatible with the maintenance of the institution of landed property in its broad outlines. Now, the reforms which are proposed on the subject of primogeniture, and of entails and settlements, are of a different character. Instead of limiting, they would increase the power over the land of the existing generation of landowners; and accordingly, the supporters of more drastic changes are much divided as to whether these particular measures ought or ought not to be supported.

Among the reasons for getting rid of the law of primogeniture and the existing laws of entail and settlement, the one which we oftenest hear, and which carries most weight with many of the assailants of those laws, is that, by keeping land out of the market, they detain it in too few hands, and that their abolition would increase the number of landed proprietors. The long and obstinate prejudice which existed against peasant properties, grounded on the densest ignorance of their actual operation in the countries where they prevail, has given way before more correct information. Those who fancied that peasant proprietors must be wretched cultivators because cottier tenants are so, have learnt that some of the best agriculture in the world is to be found where such properties abound: those who thought that peasant proprietorship breeds over-population, and converts a country into a "pauper-warren," now know that its tendency is rather towards the other extreme. Within a few years, therefore, the existence of peasant properties has come to be regarded by English philanthropists as eminently desirable, and the removal of all obstacles to it has become an aim of advanced politicians; and primogeniture and entail being such obstacles, their abolition is advocated on that ground. But it has come to pass that the same thing which recommends this measure to one class of land reformers, renders another class worse than indifferent to it. Multiplication of proprietors is not the kind of reform which finds favour with a large section of the more thorough-going land reformers. Many of them believe that an addition to the number of private owners of land is but an addition to the number of the enemies of the larger changes which they meditate. They think, and in this they are not mistaken, that the wide diffusion of landed property in some Continental countries, and especially in France, is in these countries the great obstacle to any improvement in the conditions of ownership: and they look with no good will on anything which tends, in ever so small a degree, to approximate, in this respect, the British state of things to the French.

We agree, to a considerable extent, with the general views on which this judgment is grounded; but we do not think that the question of abolishing primogeniture and entail is a case for their application. Whether the creation of a class of peasant-proprietors would be a good thing or a bad, we are of opinion that the reforms in question would not have that effect; while they would produce benefits which, even from the exclusive point of view of the land-reformers, might well outweigh some amount of the inconvenience they apprehend.

To what extent these measures would practically operate in causing land to be brought into the market, it is very difficult at present to foresee; but there is no probability that, of such as might be sold, much would come into the hands of small proprietors. As long as the private wealth of the country and its social condition are what they are, the rich will always outbid the poor in the land market. We are speaking, of course, of rural land, of which alone the possession is an object of desire to the wealthy classes. Land in towns, or so close to them as to be available for streets, might often obtain a higher price in small lots; such lots as would enable prudent and economical working people to become the owners of the houses they live in; which we hold to be an unqualified good: nor is it likely that even the most extreme plans of land reform would disturb such persons in the possession. The land of the country at large outside the towns might possibly come to be shared among a greater number of rich families than at present; but sales by the rich to the rich do not really add to the number of those whose interests and feelings are engaged on the side of landlordism; for the rich who wish to be landlords are already as much wedded to landlord privileges as they would be when they actually became so. Reformers, therefore, either moderate or extreme, need have no fear that the facilitation of the sale of land already appropriated should raise up additional obstacles to their projects.

On the other hand, the measures in question would be attended with no small amount of positive benefit. In the first place, whatever transfers of landed property might really be occasioned by these changes would be in the direction of agricultural improvement. True it is that, according to the present ideas of landed property, landlords are neither required nor expected to do anything for the land; but some landlords are more disposed to do so than others; and the purchasers are almost always a more improving class of landowners than those from whom they purchase. It is the capitalist and man of business who buys; it is the needy and the spendthrift who sell. The whole tendency is thus to improve the cultivation and increase the produce of the country. But there is a still greater benefit than this, and one which is often not sufficiently appreciated. The *principle* of the laws of primogeniture and entail is radically wrong; and to get rid of a bad principle, and put a better in its place, is equivalent to a very considerable amount of practical gain. The preference of one child above all the rest, without any superiority of personal claims, is an injustice. The power given to an owner of property to exercise control over it after it has passed into the hands of those to whom it devolves on his death, is, as a rule (with certain obvious exceptions), both an injustice and an absurdity. Moreover, the end for which these institutions are kept up ought to be their sufficient condemnation in the eyes of advanced reformers. The purpose of their existence is to retain the land, not only in the families which now possess it, but in a certain line of succession within those families, from eldest son to eldest son. They are a contrivance for maintaining an aristocratical order in unimpaired territorial wealth from generation to generation, in spite of the faults which its existing members may commit, and at the sacrifice both of justice between the heir and the other children, and of the interest which all the existing members of the family may have in selling the land. The aristocratic spirit, more powerful than the personal interest of each living member of the body, postpones the private wishes of the existing generation to the interest of the order in maintaining an aristocratic monopoly of the land. The possession of the land is the centre round which aristocratic feeling revolves; and the removal of the two props of the monopoly, though its immediate practical effect would probably be small, should be welcome to all who wish to dissolve the connexion between landed property and aristocratic institutions.

We think, then, that all land reformers, whatever may be their ulterior views, should unite in supporting the abrogation of the law of primogeniture and the reform of the law of settlement. We must reserve for another article our reasons for thinking quite otherwise of the proposal recently broached (and which has derived importance from the strong advocacy of the *Times* and from the interpretation put upon a speech of Mr. Goschen) for requiring all corporate bodies and endowed institutions to part with their lands by sale to private individuals.

J. S. MILL.

Should Public Bodies be required to Sell their Lands?

A considerable sensation seems to have been excited by the quite unexpected appearance a few weeks ago, in the *Times*, of two articles strenuously contending that corporate bodies and endowed institutions should no longer be permitted to withhold land from the market, and that the principle of the Mortmain Acts should be so far extended as to compel all such bodies or institutions to sell their lands and invest the proceeds in Government securities. The coincidence of this manifestation by the *Times* with a speech of Mr. Goschen, some expressions in which were supposed to point to a similar conclusion, has led to a suspicion that the Government is throwing out feelers preparatory to some actual proposal of the kind suggested. And the papers that are bitterly hostile to the present Government, whenever its political and social policy is other than that of keeping things as they are, have not missed the opportunity of upbraiding the Government with making an unworthy concession to the land tenure reformers, who are represented as grasping at the opportunity of attacking landed property at its most easily assailable point.

It is an odd supposition that reformers who are asserted to have, and some of whom really have, for their object the extinguishing of private and hereditary landed property altogether, desire to begin their operations by making a great mass of landed property private and hereditary which was not so before. Nothing could be more opposed to the principles and purposes of thoroughgoing land tenure reformers of every shade of opinion than any further conversion of what is still, in some sense, a kind of public property, into private. The point on which they are all agreed, whether they desire anything further or not, is that, at all events, the appropriation of the land of the country by private individuals and families has gone far enough; and that a determined resistance should be made to any further extension of it, either by the stealing, euphemistically termed the inclosure, of commons, or by the alienation of lands held upon trust for public or semi-public objects. Far from allowing any land which is not already private property to become so, the most moderate of these land reformers think that it may possibly be expedient, in districts where land not already appropriated does not abound, to redeem some part of that which is in private hands, by re-purchasing it on account of the State.

Those countries are fortunate, or would be fortunate if decently governed, in which, as in a great part of the East, the land has not been allowed to become the permanent property of individuals, and the State consequently is the sole landlord. So far as the public expenditure is covered by the proceeds of the land, those countries are untaxed; for it is the same thing as being untaxed, to pay to the State only what would have to be paid to private landlords if the land were appropriated. The principle that the land belongs to the Sovereign, and that the expenses of Government should be defrayed by it, is recognised in the theory of our own ancient institutions. The nearest thing to an absolute proprietor whom our laws know of is the freeholder, who is a tenant of the Crown; bound originally to personal service, in the field or at the plough, and, when that obligation was remitted, subject to a land tax intended to be equivalent to it. The first claim of the State has been foregone; the second has for two centuries been successfully evaded: but the original wrongdoers have been so long in their graves, and so much of the land has come into the hands of new possessors, who have bought it with their earnings at a price calculated on the unjust exemption, that the resumption of the land without indemnity would be correcting one injustice by another, while, if weighted with due compensation, it would be a measure of very doubtful profit to the State. But, though the State cannot replace itself in the fortunate condition in which it would now have been if it had reserved to itself from the beginning the whole rent of the land, this is no reason why it should go on committing the same mistake, and deprive itself of that natural increase of the rent which the possessors derive from the mere progress of wealth and population, without any exertion or sacrifice of their own. If the Grosvenor, Portman, and Portland estates belonged to the municipality of London, the gigantic incomes of those estates would probably suffice for the whole expense of the local government of the capital. But these gigantic incomes are still swelling; by the growth of London they may again be doubled, in as short a time as they have doubled already: and what have the possessors done, that this increase of wealth, produced by other people's labour and enterprise, should fall into their mouths as they sleep, instead of being applied to the public necessities of those who created it? It is maintained, therefore, by land reformers, that special taxation may justly be levied upon landed property, up to, though not exceeding, this unearned increase; excess being guarded against by leaving the possessors free to cede their land to the State at the price they could sell it for at the time when the tax is imposed, but no higher price to be claimable on account of any increase of value afterwards, unless proved to have been the effect of improvements made at the landlord's expense. Now, if the nation would be justified in thus reasserting its claim to the unearned increase of value, even when it has allowed the legal right to that increase to pass into the hands of individuals; how much more ought it to prevent further legal rights of this description from being acquired by those who do not now possess them? The landed estates of public bodies are not family property; the interest that any individual has in them is never more than a life interest, often much less; the increase of value by lapse of time would go to enrich nobody knows whom, and its appropriation by the State would give no one the shadow of a moral title to compensation. But if these lands are sold to individuals, they become hereditary, and can only be repurchased by the State at their full value as a perpetuity.

Neither would this compulsory sale be attended with any of the advantages in the form of increased production, which would result from facilitating the voluntary sale of land by individual to individual. As long as, by the theory and practice of landed proprietorship, the landlord of an estate is a mere sinecurist quartered on it, improvement by the landlord is an accident dependent on his personal tastes. But he who sells his land, voluntarily or from necessity, is almost always below the average of landlords in disposition and ability to improve; the tendency of the change of proprietors is, therefore, in favour of improvement. But there is no reason to think that public bodies in general are worse than average landlords in any particular ; it is matter of common remark that they are less grasping: and, if they do not come up to the most enterprising landlords in what they themselves accomplish, they leave more power of improvement, and more encouragement to it, to their tenants, than the majority of private landlords. It would, therefore, be no gain, but all loss, to reinforce the enemies of the reform of landed tenure by the addition of a new class of wealthy hereditary landholders, quartered upon land which is as yet devoted more or less faithfully to public uses. If public bodies are required to part with their lands, they should part with them to the State, and to that alone.

Whether it is desirable that such bodies should be holders of lands; whether it is wise that their time and attention should be divided between their appointed duties, certain to be enforced with increasing strictness as improvement goes on, and the management of a tenantry, with the duties which, if private property in land continues to exist, are sure to be more and more attached to it,—is a question of the future, which it may be left to the future to decide. We do not think it can be properly decided until the fermentation now going on in the public mind, respecting the constitution of landed property, has subsided into a definite conviction respecting the end to be aimed at, and the means of practically drawing nearer to that end. But the time has come for announcing with the utmost decision, and we hope to see land reformers uniting as one body in the demand, that no private appropriation of land not yet private property shall hereafter take place under any circumstances or on any pretext. J. S. MILL.

Examiner, Jan. 11th, 1873.

Mr. Bright has sent the following letter, written by the late Mr. Cobden nine years ago, for republication in the *Daily News* :—

"All ancient legislators, especially Moses, grounded the success of their ordinances concerning virtue, justice, and morality upon securing hereditary estates, or, at least, landed property, to the greatest possible number of citizens."— Niebuhr.

"At the annual meeting of the Romsey Labourers' Encouragement Association, the Hon. William Cowper, who presided in the absence of Lord Palmerston, in alluding to the 'disadvantages and privations to which the agricultural labourer is exposed,' is reported to have said:— 'I do not allude to such imaginary grievances as that of the tillers of the soil having any share in the ownership of the land. Such a complaint as that rests upon a fallacy and a delusion. If it were possible to make the labourers the owners of the land which they are tilling it would be a retrograde movement in agriculture. The great progress in agriculture of late years has been due to the concentration and application of capital to an amount of land which is sufficient to justify the favourable employment of that capital ; and it would be going back to times of less prosperity —it would be following the example of countries less prosperous than England in agriculture—if we were to aim at such an absurd and impossible object. (Hear, hear.)'

"The above argument may be called generic, for it expresses the views of the class which have possession of the soil of this country. Lord Palmerston gave utterance to similar opinions, on Mr. Maguire's motion in the House, when he deprecated any change which should 'reduce the occupiers of the Irish soil' to the condition of the French peasant proprietors ; and it is not reported that there was a roar of laughter at this grim joke.

" Now nobody has, I believe, proposed that we should adopt in England the French law of succession; but it pleases those who are the advocates of the land laws of this country to bring forward the peasant proprietor of France as a sort of ' Old Bogy' to frighten us into the love of our own feudal system. This compels those who desire any amelioration of the present system to meet them on their own ground. I propose, with your permission, and with the aid of such high authorities as I shall cite, to offer to your readers the materials for forming a judgment upon the state and prospects of the peasant proprietary of France.

" Two questions are presented to us in connexion with this subject—What are the moral, and what are the economical effects produced by the division of the land of a country among its whole people? In France, Switzerland, Norway, Germany, Belgium, the Channel Islands, and in the United States the land is, as a rule, the property of those who cultivate it. The same state of things prevails more or less, or is being rapidly developed, in Italy, Spain, Russia, Hungary, and other countries. England is the only great country where feudalism still rules the destinies of the land, and where the owners of the soil are constantly diminishing in number. I will, however, confine myself to France, because it is the country where the system under consideration may be said to have originated, and which furnishes an example on the largest scale of extreme and uniform division of land, and because, being the country most often referred to in condemnation of the system, and from its proximity and the high character of the authorities to be quoted, it affords the most satisfactory materials for forming a correct judgment on the matter.

"Now, looking at the moral aspect of the question alone, nobody will deny the advantages which the possession of landed property must confer upon a man or a body of men—that it imparts a higher sense of independence and security, greater self-respect, and supplies stronger motives for industry, frugality, and forethought than any other kind of property. But we have not to weigh the various moral influences produced by the ownership of different kinds of property. The question really is between owning land or possessing nothing; for in proclaiming that the whole class of agricultural labourers must for ever abandon the hope or ambition of becoming landowners, they are virtually told that they can never emerge from the condition of weekly labourers; for the tillers of the earth can, as a class, rise to wealth only by sharing in the possession of the soil. Let us see to what proportion of the agricultural population this proscription extends.

"By the last census tables of the occupations of the people it appears that in England and Wales there are, in round numbers, 15,100 landed proprietors and 1,100,000 farm labourers. The classification of the proprietors may be wanting in accuracy, but it is enough to know that, taking the whole United Kingdom, while the owners of the soil are reckoned by thousands, its cultivators must be counted by millions. The farmers and graziers in England and Wales, 220,000 in number, have in a vast majority of cases no property in the land they occupy, but as it is not yet proposed to put them under the ban of perpetual exclusion from the class of proprietors, the moral aspect of the question does not affect them to the same extent as the labourers. Now, the whole question as between the millions of peasant proprietors in France and the millions of farm labourers in England is summed up in a few words by M. Passy, in a small volume entitled *Des Systèmes de Culture en France, et de leur Influence sur l'Economie Sociale,* which should be read by all who take an interest in this question. 'As for the idea, so often reproduced,' says he, ' that large farms contribute more than small to the welfare of the population employed on them, it scarcely deserves notice. The whole difference between the two systems is that, in the one case, there are few masters and many hired labourers—in the other, more masters and fewer hired labourers. Now, should not that be a sufficient reason for preferring the latter?' Bearing in mind that, in speaking of small farms, M. Passy means small freeholds, can we doubt, were his question put to the British peasant instead of the landowner, what his answer would be?

"But upon the moral aspect of the question there cannot be two opinions, and therefore it does not admit of controversy. On the Continent the verdict on this view of the question is unanimously in favour of small landed properties; and, unless we in England are insincere in the arguments we address to the working classes to induce them to become depositors in saving banks, or to enter the ranks of distributors and producers by means of 'co-operation,' we shall also admit that to become a small freeholder would elevate the labouring man in the scale of society. This has been proved by experience on the largest scale in France, where five millions of landed proprietors, every one a voter, constitute the foundation of the social and political edifice, and of whom rulers and orators delight to speak as the pride and safeguard of the State. If we would realize the contrast presented by the abject condition of our own peasantry, it is afforded by such incidents as that of the speaker at the above-named meeting telling his patronized audience (and his audience listening acquiescingly !) that for them the acquisition of a plot of land was 'an absurd and impossible object,' or by a recent picture in *Punch*, where, on the occasion of a hint having been uttered that land and votes might be possessed by the same class in England as in France, the British peasant was caricatured in a form which conveyed the impression of a cross between an Aztec and a New Zealander.

" But it is on the second or economical branch of the subject—namely, the effect of small landed properties on the progress of scientific agriculture that the great controversy really arises. Can what is called high farming be carried on successfully where the land is cultivated by peasant proprietors? It might almost be a sufficient answer to say that the highest standard of agriculture is horticulture, which is always conducted on a diminutive scale. This, however, would be to evade the major part of the question, whether, on small properties, farming can be pursued with the same economy as on large—whether the net proceeds, after deducting the cost of production, can be as great in the one case as the other. On this point the influential public opinion of England has been resolutely on the side of great farms. Not content with preferring our own system, we have, as is our English wont, passed summary condemnation on those who have not conformed to our standard.

Mr. M'Culloch, with his usual dogmatism, took a prominent part, nearly forty years ago, in denouncing the division of land as it is practised by our neighbours, predicting that, if it were continued for another half century, ' France would become the greatest pauper warren in Europe.' Thirty years after this rash prophecy M. Passy publishes a second edition of his *Systèmes de Culture*, in which the important question is discussed in all its aspects. M. Passy was a peer of France under Louis Philippe, and afterwards filled the post of Minister of Finance. He is a considerable landed proprietor, and ranks as one of the most distinguished political economists of France. It would be difficult to find a person combining higher qualifications for his task, and the result of his investigations is a decided preference, on economical, social, and moral grounds, of the French system to that of this country. He shows, as indeed all the accredited French authorities show, that the evils of the subdivision of land, as it is practically carried out in France, are much exaggerated, indeed, caricatured, by its opponents; that the enforced division of the property of a deceased parent among his children does not necessarily involve the partition of the land; that arrangements are often made by which one of the family takes the estate, paying to the co-heirs a compensation in money, or the whole is sold and the proceeds are divided; and thus, as the government statistics prove, the separate landed properties of France are not increasing in number in proportion to the increase of the population—in short, experience shows, as common sense might have foreseen, that as men do not cut up their cloth or leather to waste, so neither will they, as a rule, subdivide that which is far more precious—the land —into useless fragments.

" M. Passy gives us the following deductions as the result of his investigations :—' 1. That in the present state of agricultural knowledge and practice, it is the small farms (*la petite culture*) which, after deducting the cost of production, yields from a given surface, and on equal conditions, the greatest net produce; and, 2nd, that the same system of cultivation, by maintaining a larger rural population, not only thereby adds to the strength of a State, but affords a better market for those commodities the production and exchange of which stimulate the prosperity of the manufacturing districts.'

"This conclusion, so opposed to the doctrine current in this country, is confirmed by the highest authorities in France, as well as by those English writers who, whether as occasional residents in that country or as travellers—such as Mill, Inglis, Kay, &c.—have had the best opportunities of forming a correct judgment on the matter. And it should be added that these views have been constantly gaining ground in France during the last half-century, until they have almost ceased to be a subject of controversy in that country. And surely if any one circumstance be more calculated than another to impose a modest diffidence on even the most conservative of British critics, it is the high social and intellectual position of those Frenchmen who are the advocates of the system of peasant properties. This task is not left to the Red Republicans or the ultra-Democrats. Men of exalted rank and noble birth, who might be excused for feeling some repugnance to a social organization which has to a large extent been erected upon the ruins of their class—the descendants of those whose families were scattered or who perished on the scaffold during the Revolution—have been among the most able and earnest champions of the present order of things. Thus M. de Tocqueville, writing in the confidence of private friendship, from the chateau in Normandy bearing his name, and surrounded by a body of peasant proprietors occupying the greater part of the ancestral domain of his family, yet speaks with hearty commendation of the change. And the present state of things finds a defender in a venerable French nobleman, who is widely known and honoured in England for the purity of his character and his high intellectual endowments—the head of the ducal house of De Broglie. The circumstance to which I am referring—the elevated character and eminent position of the advocates of the French system—seems to have had its effect on the conservative and philosophical mind of Dr. Chalmers, who visited France in 1838, imbued with Mr. M'Culloch's predilections against the division of landed property.

"Dr. Chalmers records in his diary, which has been published since his death, the conversations he had on this subject with men of the highest social and political position, whom he describes as 'intelligent and truly Conservative.' One of them, François Delessert, member of the Chamber of Deputies, Parisian merchant, tells him that he 'apprehends no harm from the subdivision of property—speaks of the checks to it—that it is greatly overrated—that family arrangements often prevent it.' But a conversation with a nobleman, already mentioned, seems to have produced the greatest impression on his mind, as will be seen by the following extract from his diary :—' June 21, 1838.— Duke de Broglie made a very able defence of the French law of succession, and said (*inter alia*) that the minutely subdivided land on the Seine was, before, not cultivated at all. At Lille, he says, there is first-rate agriculture in large farms from small properties pieced together. That in the canton of Berne, one part, under the law of primogeniture, has large properties, splendid houses, admirable agriculture, but a population supported by a poor-rate. Another part, under the law of equal division, has a worse agriculture, and a better conditioned population without a pauper among them.'

"Dr. Chalmers closes his diary with these words :—' A most interesting journey, by which my opinion of the actual state of property in France, and also my views of the eventual, have been made more favourable. Much, however, must be left to time and experience. I have been greatly enlightened by the conversation of the Duke de Broglie.'

"A few years after Dr. Chalmers's tour in France, the agricultural districts of that country were visited by Mr. Henry Coleman, professor of agriculture in Massachusetts, who was on a special mission from that State to report on the condition of agriculture in Europe. It would be difficult to find a witness more deserving of attention on the subject under consideration. The following are extracts from his published letters :—

"'At first I thought I should find nothing in French agriculture worthy of much attention, but my opinion has undergone a change, and I begin to think their agriculture not only good, but advanced. They do not grow the same productions as England; their work is not executed in so neat a manner; their implements are primitive and somewhat rude; their neat stock is less improved, and, indeed, the whole system is different; but I am disposed to believe that their farming is more economical, and that, taken as a whole, the condition of the labouring classes is superior to that of the English. . . . I have never seen a more civil, clean, well-dressed, happy set of people than the French peasantry, with scarcely an exception, and they contrast most strongly in this respect with the English and Scotch. I seldom went among a field of labourers in England or Scotland, especially if they were women, without some coarse joke or indecent leer. It is the reverse in France—the address, even of the poorest (I do not at all exaggerate) is as polite as that of the best people you find in a city; so far from soliciting money, they have refused it in repeated instances when, for some little service, I have offered some compensation. Count de Gourcy told me, again and again, that even the most humble of them would consider it an offence to have it offered them. I do not believe there ever was a happier peasantry than the French, and they are pre-eminent for their industry and economy.'

" But the most recent, and, at the same time, the highest testimony on this subject remains to be cited. M. Léonce de Lavergne is well known as one of the most accomplished, laborious, and conscientious writers on agriculture of the present age. His work, contrasting the rural economy of England, Scotland, and Ireland with that of France, published in 1850, attracted much attention at the time in this country. He has since published occasional articles in periodicals, and has edited a French translation of Arthur Young's Travels in France. But his most important work,

On the Rural Economy of France since 1789, was published about four years ago. Now, in all these works, he is the consistent, able, but discriminating advocate of the division of land as it exists in France, and as contrasted with the system which prevails in this country.

"*The Journal of the Royal Agricultural Society of England* (Vol. xxi. 1860), contains a review of the latest work of M. de Lavergne, to which I refer, not only because the *Journal* is our highest authority on practical agriculture, but because the review in question affords a truly characteristic illustration of the English mode of arguing the land question with foreigners. After speaking in the very highest terms of eulogy of M. de Lavergne's ' admirable book,' of his ' graphic descriptions,' his ' inexhaustible fund of historical, legendary, and economical illustrations,' the reviewer adds :—
' We trust we have said enough of its singular merits to induce all those who can read the French language to procure the book itself and

read it through. Let no one be deterred from doing so by its forbidding title, as we have rarely seen dry statistical facts and figures comprised in so alluring a form, and interspersed with so many entertaining details and pictures of scenery, manners and customs, &c. In one word, M. de Lavergne has written a book which has its place everywhere—in the study of the learned, in the boudoir or drawing-room of the wealthy, and especially in the travelling bag of the tourist.'

" I was very curious to see how the organ of our great agricultural society, after these well-deserved compliments, would deal with the accomplished Frenchman's views on the division of the land. 'M. de Lavergne,' says the reviewer, ' is not disposed to consider an extreme division of landed property as an obstacle to agricultural progress, and we shall presently examine the arguments by which he attempts to establish his opinion.' Accordingly, in the following page, the subject is again referred to, and we are told that 'M. de Lavergne greatly approves the equal division of property by inheritance, and certainly adduces very cogent reasons to support his views; but this is a point, and perhaps the only one, on which we do not agree with him.' And how does the reviewer proceed to 'examine the arguments' of a writer who is treating of a subject to which he has given a life of study, in a work rich with valuable statistics and historical facts, every page of which bears evidence of his ability and practical knowledge? While asserting a difference of opinion on the one capital point upon which M. de Lavergne possessed such superior sources of intelligence, the reviewer might have been expected to have adduced some facts or figures in support of his views. Nothing more, however, is deemed necessary, in the present sentimental phase of the land question, than straightway to raise the cry of 'our old nobility.' 'Few who can appreciate,' says the reviewer, 'the social and intellectual influence exercised by the aristocracy of this country, will concur with M. de Lavergne on the subject of the privilege of primogeniture.' Then follows half a page of glorification of our 'large landowners,' of their services to agriculture by 'scientific discoveries and costly experiments,' in the course of which we are told that 'there is not a single page of English history in which the aristocracy is not associated with its glorious records.' And this rhapsodical diversion from the real question at issue terminates with a dogmatical repudiation of M. de Lavergne's views respecting the division of land in France. Not one word is vouchsafed to the case of the millions of agricultural labourers in this kingdom. The moment the aristocracy is thrown into the scale, it is assumed to outweigh reason, argument, logic, and facts. What is this but a practical application of the lines :—

"' Let law and learning, trade and commerce die,
But leave us still our old nobility.'"

" We laugh at the Spaniards because, when

challenged to defend their antiquated practices, they deem it a sufficient answer to say, 'Cosas d'Espana;' but where is the difference between this and the above mode of arguing with an enlightened foreigner?

"I have said that M. de Lavergne is a discriminating advocate of the French peasant proprietors. He allows that there is room for improvement in the working of his favourite system, and that in some cases the *morcellement* of the land is too minute for agricultural purposes though it is not admitted that this is the necessary or general tendency.

"There are family arrangements which constantly tend to unite as well as to divide estates —as, for instance, the accession of property brought by marriage in a country where the habit of giving marriage-portions to daughters is universal.

"M. de Lavergne concedes to England, as a whole, the more advanced position in scientific farming, acknowledging that in the agricultural products common to both countries the average yield of our crops will be superior to that of France. This, however, is not attributable to the size of the farms, but to the earlier development of our mechanical and industrial resources —an advantage which has given us the lead not only in agriculture but in many branches of manufacturing production. He vindicates his countrymen from all discredit in this respect by pointing to the very different ordeals through which the two countries have passed since 1788, when Arthur Young made his agricultural tour in France. It is calculated that in the wars between 1792 and 1815 two millions and a half of Frenchmen perished on battle-fields or in hospitals. Laws of '*maximum*' and every conceivable violation of the rules of political economy were perpetrated. Vast masses of land wrested from the nobility, Church, and corporations passed suddenly into the hands of individuals who had neither capital nor intelligence to bring them into profitable cultivation.

The energies which might have been employed in clearing the wilderness, draining the morass, or restoring to impoverished soils their natural fertility, were exhausted on a thousand battle-fields, where the valour and genius exhibited by Frenchmen showed what would have been achieved had those qualities been devoted to the more useful and enduring conquests of peace. During those 22 years, while every institution in France was again and again fundamentally remodelled, and the monarchy, aristocracy, and Church were overthrown—while, at last, foreign armies, after marching through the country, were twice in occupation of the capital, the whole terminating with the exaction of enormous pecuniary indemnities from the prostrate nation—during all this time England, secure against internal revolution and foreign aggression, was pursuing an undisturbed career of agricultural improvement. What wonder if, under such favourable circumstances, she outstripped her neighbour in the path of progress? Ought it not rather to excite our astonishment that in less than a century the peasantry of France could bear any comparison with our own in the enjoyment of the necessaries and comforts of life? Yet, so great were the recuperative forces in the rural population of France—arising, as is maintained by her highest authorities, from the general diffusion of landed property—that in less than a quarter of a century after the peace of 1815 the English pedestrian tourist, Inglis, was enabled to pen this declaration:—' With a tolerably intimate knowledge and distinct recollection of the lower orders in France, I assert that, upon the whole, the peasantry of France are the happiest peasantry of any country in Europe.' I have trespassed too long on your space, otherwise I could adduce further testimony in favour of the system of small landed properties, particularly from the pages of Mr. Mill, who, by long study of the best authorities, and by occasional residence in France, has made himself thoroughly master of the subject. But I have preferred, as far as possible, to call as witnesses those who are technically versed in the science of agriculture. The result of a general study of all the best authorities is to show that there is an unanimity of opinion in favour of the French system, on moral grounds, as tending to elevate the character, promote the intelligence, and stimulate the industry of the peasantry. There is scarcely less agreement on the economical view, expressed by M. Passy, that small properties, 'after deducting the cost of production, yield, from a given surface, and on equal conditions, the greatest net produce.' Those 'equal conditions' can, of course, only be found by comparing corresponding specimens of the two systems. The advocates of the *petite culture*, while admitting that the average production of England exceeds that of France, contend that in Flanders (the very birthplace of scientific farming), on the Rhine, in Guernsey, Switzerland, the North of France, and other parts, farms of 15 or 20 acres may be found cultivated by their proprietors, which yield a greater net produce than the same extent of surface on the best farms in England and Scotland. M. de Lavergne says that the proprietors of 15 acres 'enjoy sometimes a real affluence.' This is more than the average size of the separate farming properties in Guernsey and Jersey, where the population are renowned for their comparative prosperity and happiness. As a proof that this division of property promotes the accumulation of wealth, without tending to the deterioration of the soil, it may be stated that farming land is worth nearly twice as much, when let or sold, in Guernsey as in England. It is contended, moreover, that at the present moment the peasant proprietors are making more rapid progress in improvement than the ordinary renting farmer without a lease, owing to the greater stimulus imparted by what Arthur Young designated the 'magic of property.'

"The partisans of the French system look to 'co-operation' as a means of remedying whatever defects or evils may be found to arise from a too minute subdivision of the land. This principle, which has already been resorted to by our own intelligent workpeople as a means of elevating themselves to the class of shopkeepers and manufacturers, is peculiarly adapted to meet the case of the small agriculturists. It is a fallacy to suppose that the little proprietor must necessarily be a small farmer, in the usual sense of the term. A number of adjoining properties may be united into a large farm. In England the ordinary tenant of a few hundred acres does not keep his own steam-engine or thrashing-machine. They are hired out from farm to farm. There is no reason why the drilling-machine, the horse-hoe, the roller, or the clod-crusher, should not make its rounds in a similar way. Already, we are told, the principle of association is applied to cheese-making and other branches of agriculture on the Continent. The practice will extend and, with the increase of intelligence, it may prove the solution of the problem, and remove every difficulty in the way of the successful cultivation of peasant properties.

"But I have said enough, probably, to assist your readers to an appreciation of the question before us. That question has been raised, not by those who desire some relaxation of our feudal land code, but by those who would deter us from any change, by pointing to the terrible law of succession in France. I offer no opinion for or against that law. But if the peasant proprietors, who are its offspring, are to be paraded at our 'labourers' encouragement associations,' to frighten those thralls of the nineteenth century—the essential innovation in whose fortunes, since the days of the Gurths and Wambas of the Middle Ages, is the transfer of their allegiance from the castle to the "Union"—is there no danger that, like their rooks, they may learn to look the scarecrow in the face, and that some Romsey Hampden may find a voice and exclaim, 'Let un come! Who be afeard?'

"Jan. 22, 1864."

Times, Jan. 7th, 1873.

F.

There is a great peer at this moment who happens not to be a spending man, and saves about £100,000 a year—this is an under-statement—which he invests in Scotch landed property. He buys great bits of country as they come into the market—a third of one county is his already—and he uses his purchases for two ends, first to make enormous clearances in order to protect deer, and secondly, to obtain influence over elections. What does it matter to him if he does not take the highest rent obtainable for his territory? What does it matter if he does not get any price at all? What does it matter if it costs him half his savings annually to carry out his own will? If his entire Scotch property cost him £50,000 a year of sheer direct cash loss, and he kept his absolutism, he would be a more important man in the Empire than if he had a Scotch rent-roll of £50,000, and no more power over his tenants than he has over his tenants in the capital. He wants power, not money, and free contract granted, he will have power, and every millionaire with brains and without philanthropies, every man with two millions in his treasury, clear ideas of English life, and the principles of the *Pall Mall Gazette's* correspondent " F.," may follow his example. We say deliberately, that supposing Arran saleable—it is protected, we believe, by some entailing statute—it would pay any man with two millions to give double the survey value of the island, and let every tenant live rent-free for ever—that is, to sacrifice a million—on condition that his political orders should be implicitly obeyed. He would be a bigger man in the Empire, and philanthropy apart, a happier man than if he kept his cash fortune entire.

G.

" It was perhaps in accordance with the Malthusian maxims of the day (1816), that the Marquis of Stafford, who had become by marriage

Lord of Sutherland, determined to transport the whole population on his estate of 800,000 acres from the interior to the seashore. In two or three years the work was complete. To make room for thirty-nine sheep-farmers and their five or six shepherds, fifteen thousand herdsmen or small farmers were either driven out of the country, or settled on the seashore, on lots of two acres of unreclaimed land, at 2s. 6d. the acre of rent, on seven years' lease. Though we are told this was alone sufficient for their comfortable support — a statement as evidently incorrect as the one that corn could not be advantageously grown in the interior—they were ordered to betake themselves to the herring fishing. The trade of a fisherman, especially in those northern seas, is uncertain, laborious, and peculiarly dangerous to a novice. Yet the people, poor, uninstructed, and ignorant of the English language, had little choice of their own destiny. In spite of their entreaties, protestations, and passive resistance, they were compelled to build their huts upon the shore, and take the small lots provided for them. The other proprietors imitated the example of the 'Lord of Sutherland,' and chased out their tenants, without however assigning any provision for their future support. Almost the whole of the great county of Sutherland was reduced to a wilderness, tenanted only by sheep, with one shepherd to the square mile."

Schön well knew the religious fervour of Stein, and probed his tender point in a letter, 16th August, 1810, upon the question of paper money, &c., &c.

It appears that Stein was a great admirer of Wilberforce.

"'When the decrees of Providence are about to be fulfilled, and Governments begin to totter, we cannot say that such and such a person occasions their decay. Every one carries fuel to the flame. Heaven is far above intellect, and reasoning can only follow the event. Thus says the pious Wilberforce as an observer of what was then taking place, and as a prophet of that which was to come. This is the only explanation of the fact that the man, firm as a rock, with a pure and noble will, (Stein) could send a message, that occasioned much prosperity indeed, but for the most part annihilated or rendered insecure that which the Dane (Niebuhr) and the Prussian (Schön) were on the point of accomplishing. Both plainly said, Paper money and people, specie and bank, land and duty, rate and contract, can only lead to death. The Dane, the mild Dane, was exasperated to that degree that he warned the gentleman (Stein), of course respectfully, but firmly, and thus brought hate and enmity upon himself. The Prussian also did his duty, and now apparently the Dane and the Prussian are about to return to their homes. Both, however, will state openly what they have done."

This roused Stein thoroughly. On the 29th August he answered :—

" Most probably Wilberforce would have made answer to the Dane and Prussian who wish to return to their homes, ' that he only can boast of having fought the good fight, who remains till the end of the battle.' Wilberforce would cry, ' Watch ye, stand fast in the faith, quit you like men,' 1 Cor. iv. 20, and again, ' For the Kingdom of God is not in word, but in power,' 1 Cor. iv. 20 ; and again, ' Let no man seek his own, but every man another's *wealth*,' 1 Cor. x. 24.

" Moreover, Wilberforce would have quoted the whole passage relating to the love of a sorrowing Fatherland and an unfortunate King, and especially verse 4, ' Charity suffereth long and is kind; charity envieth not ;' and also verse 7, ' Beareth all things, believeth all things, hopeth all things, endureth all things ;' and further, ' Charity edifieth,' 1 Cor. viii. 1. And now as to the remark that paper money and peoples, &c., lead to death, I have to observe— Is there any other course open in a case of cancer or gangrene, than to have recourse to the knife, hemlock, or caustic? Would you attempt a cure by putting on a simple dressing? Paper money is an evil, and oppressive measures to raise money are also evils. But the present state of things is a more grievous evil still, and to allow them to continue would be yet more grievous. Who would ever reproach Frederick the Great for having uttered base coin, when the alternative was the destruction of the State? And by the same reasoning the present emission of an excessive paper currency is to be defended, particularly when we regard it as a means of resisting the continued efforts of a foreign power.'»

Stein wrote thus on the 29th August, but in the following September he was obliged to acknowledge that Schön was right, and that the issue of paper money was very questionable.

Notwithstanding this, he still retained his resentment against Schön and Niebuhr, and complained that the latter wished to make himself appear as a " martyr to truth."

THE END.

LONDON
PRINTED BY KERBY AND ENDEAN,
190, OXFORD STREET.

www.ingramcontent.com/pod-product-compliance
Lightning Source LLC
Chambersburg PA
CBHW021727220426
43662CB00008B/745